PENGUIN CLASSICS

POEMS OF THE NIGHT

JORGE LUIS BORGES was born in Buenos Aires in 1899 and was educated in Europe. One of the most widely acclaimed writers of our time, he published many collections of poems, essays, and short stories before his death in Geneva in June 1986. In 1961, Borges shared the International Publisher's Prize with Samuel Beckett. The Ingram Merrill Foundation granted him its Annual Literary Award in 1966 for his "outstanding contribution to literature." In 1971, Columbia University awarded him the first of many degrees of Doctor of Letters, *honoris causa* (eventually the list included both Oxford and Cambridge), that he was to receive from the English-speaking world. In 1971, he also received the fifth biennial Jerusalem Prize and in 1973 was given one of Mexico's most prestigious cultural awards, the Alfonso Reyes Prize. In 1980, he shared with Gerardo Diego the Cervantes Prize, the highest literary accolade in the Spanish-speaking world. Borges was director of the Argentine National Library from 1955 until 1973.

EFRAÍN KRISTAL is a professor of Spanish and comparative literature at UCLA and the author of *Invisible Work: Borges and Translation* and *Temptation of the Word: The Novels of Mario Vargas Llosa.*

SUZANNE JILL LEVINE, the distinguished translator of such innovative Spanish American writers as Manuel Puig, Guillermo Cabrera Infante, Jorge Luis Borges, and Julio Cortázar, is the author of *The Subversive Scribe: Translating Latin American Fiction* and *Manuel Puig and the Spider Woman: His Life and Fictions.* A professor of Latin American literature and translation studies at the University of California at Santa Barbara, she has been awarded PEN American Center and PEN USA West awards, National Endowment for the Arts and for the Humanities grants, and a Guggenheim Foundation fellowship.

The Translators

Robert Fitzgerald
Kenneth Krabbenhoft
Anthony Kerrigan
Stephen Kessler
John King
Suzanne Jill Levine
Eric McHenry
Christopher Maurer
W. S. Merwin
Alastair Reid
Hoyt Rogers
Charles Tomlinson
Alan S. Trueblood
John Updike

JORGE LUIS BORGES

Poems of the Night

A DUAL-LANGUAGE EDITION
WITH PARALLEL TEXT

Edited with an Introduction and Notes by
EFRAÍN KRISTAL

General Editor
SUZANNE JILL LEVINE

PENGUIN BOOKS

PENGUIN BOOKS

Published by the Penguin Group

Penguin Group (USA) Inc., 375 Hudson Street, New York, New York 10014, U.S.A.

Penguin Group (Canada), 90 Eglinton Avenue East, Suite 700, Toronto,
Ontario, Canada M4P 2Y3 (a division of Pearson Penguin Canada Inc.)

Penguin Books Ltd, 80 Strand, London WC2R 0RL, England

Penguin Ireland, 25 St Stephen's Green, Dublin 2, Ireland (a division of Penguin Books Ltd)

Penguin Group (Australia), 250 Camberwell Road, Camberwell,
Victoria 3124, Australia (a division of Pearson Australia Group Pty Ltd)

Penguin Books India Pvt Ltd, 11 Community Centre, Panchsheel Park, New Delhi – 110 017, India

Penguin Group (NZ), 67 Apollo Drive, Rosedale, North Shore 0632,
New Zealand (a division of Pearson New Zealand Ltd)

Penguin Books (South Africa) (Pty) Ltd, 24 Sturdee Avenue,
Rosebank, Johannesburg 2196, South Africa

Penguin Books Ltd, Registered Offices:
80 Strand, London WC2R 0RL, England

First published in Penguin Books 2010

1   3   5   7   9   10   8   6   4   2

LIBRARY OF CONGRESS CATALOGING IN PUBLICATION DATA

Borges, Jorge Luis, 1899–1986.

[Poems. English & Spanish. Selections]

Poems of the night : a dual-language edition with parallel text / Jorge Luis Borges ; edited with
an introduction and notes by Efraín Kristal ; general editor, Suzanne Jill Levine.

p. cm. — (Penguin classics)

This collection brings together Borges' poetic meditations on nighttime, darkness, and the
crepuscular world of visions and dreams, many poems appear here in English for the first time.

Includes bibliographical references and index.

ISBN 978-0-14-310600-5

1. Night—Poetry.   2. Borges, Jorge Luis, 1899–1986—Translations into English.
I. Kristal, Efraín, 1959–   II. Levine, Suzanne Jill.   III. Title.

PQ7797.B635A2 2010a
861'.62—dc22

Printed in the United States of America
Set in Sabon

Contents

POEMS OF THE NIGHT

Introduction

In the prologue to his final collection, *Los conjurados* (1985), Jorge Luis Borges declares that some of the poems came to him in dreams, and he calls them "gifts of the night, or more precisely, of the dawn."[1] Sixty years earlier, soon after publishing his second book of poems—*Moon Across the Way* (1925)—Borges observed that our lyrical core is "poetry of the night and the penumbra."[2] The Spanish literary critic Vicente Cervera Salinas is one of many readers of Borges to observe that "the night might well be the emblem of his poetry."[3] Throughout his career as poet, Borges returned to the night, the dark, and the crepuscular world of visions and dreams, themes that speak to the blindness that would overtake him slowly, over a long period of time: "that slow nightfall, that slow loss of sight, began when I began to see. It has continued without dramatic moments, a slow nightfall that has lasted more than three quarters of a century. In 1955, the pathetic moment came when I knew I had lost my sight, my reader's and writer's sight."[4]

Poems of the Night gathers Borges's most eloquent signature poems—among them "The Cyclical Night," "The Moon," "History of the Night," and "Poem of the Gifts"—along with lesser-known poems; whether famous or unknown, they all share oneiric moments, explorations of sleep or insomnia, and meditations on death and blindness. While many of the translations have been previously published, twenty-two of the more than fifty poems collected here were translated especially for this book, and some appear in English for the first time. These include "Insomnia" (1921), one of Borges's earliest poems, which illustrates that night was central to his poetry even as he experimented with a jagged avant-garde style he would soon leave behind, and "The Gift" (1985), one of his last, published in a Uruguayan literary journal shortly before his death.

While Borges the fabulist is known to readers everywhere, many are unaware that he is also a major Latin American poet. He began writing poetry during World War I as a teenager living with his family in Geneva, reading Walt Whitman and Heinrich Heine with enthusiasm, and translating German expressionist poems. After a formative stint in Spain, where he was caught up in the avant-garde whirlwind, he returned to Argentina in the 1920s and wrote poetry that combined the geography (and even the history) of the Río de la Plata region of his birth with a metaphysical aura that would surround most of his subsequent literary works, and that rehearsed many of his characteristic motifs—the mirror, labyrinth, cyclical time, and infinity. These, he admitted on several occasions, were the products of his nightmares:

> I have two nightmares that often become confused with each other. I have the nightmare of the labyrinth, which comes, in part, from a steel engraving I saw in a French book when I was a child. In this engraving were the Seven Wonders of the World, among them the labyrinth of Crete. I believed when I was a child (or I now believe I believed) that if one had a magnifying glass powerful enough, one could look through the cracks and see the Minotaur in the terrible center of the labyrinth. My other nightmare is that of a mirror. The two are not distinct, as it takes only two facing mirrors to construct a labyrinth. I always dream of labyrinths or of mirrors. In the dream of the mirror another vision appears, another terror of my nights, and that is the idea of the mask. Masks have always scared me. No doubt I felt in my childhood that someone who was wearing a mask was hiding something horrible. These are my most terrible nightmares: I see myself reflected in a mirror, but the reflection is wearing a mask. I am afraid to pull the mask off, afraid to see my real face.[5]

In the 1930s, Borges wrote several poems (including the cele-brated "Dreamtigers" of 1934) that would point to the beginning of a new and exciting direction in his poetry akin to the mature vision that would later inform his best-known fictions. In 1938, however, after suffering a hospitalization due to a head concus-sion that almost cost him his life, Borges considerably reduced his output of new poems. He decided to practice the short story, the genre that would establish his literary fame, even though he always considered it a minor, less rigorous form. But he did not abandon poetry altogether. The 1943, 1953, and 1958 editions of his collected poetry include many revisions of his earlier works and several new remarkable poems, including "The Cyclical Night," "The Golem," and "Of Heaven and Hell." It is likely that in the 1940s and 1950s he worked on some poems he never published, and on others that were not quite ready for publica-tion. But after *The Maker* (1960), and for the rest of his life, he published poems on a regular basis. The range of his themes expanded considerably, drawing on many literary traditions, in-cluding Nordic mythology and short Japanese forms. By then he had also lost his "reader's and writer's sight" and began to make up poems in his mind:

> I always do my first drafts walking up and down the street. When I find that I'm apt to forget, I dictate what I have. If I don't do that I'm hampered by the fact of having to keep it in my memory. Then I go on, shaping and reshaping.[6]

Poems of the Night came about from a similar process of shap-ing and reshaping. Borges was a man of wide-ranging interests, and in his poetry he created a literary self who dons different masks and whose lyrical mind ranges widely. He would often make whimsical remarks about his indifference to the thematic, or even the formal unity of his poetry collections. He would say, for instance, that he was happy his Argentine editor agreed to publish another book of his poems every time he could come up with at least thirty new ones. It amused him when critics com-plained that short prose pieces in his collections struck them as compact narrative fiction, autobiographical notes, or concise essays, rather than true poems.[7] He would sometimes caution his readers not to confuse the suggestive title of any one of his books with the main theme of his motley assortments. The following cautionary note is representative: "This book is only a compilation. Each poem, written in response to different moods and moments, was not designed to form part of a book."[8]

In *Fervor de Buenos Aires* (1923), for example, the lion's share of the poems are crepuscular visions of the Argentine capital, in which Borges's poetic voice sings ruefully but with Whitmanesque pride in those moments when day turns to night, and night to dawn.[9] Still, Borges does not exclude poems whose themes diverge from this, including "Benares," surely inspired by the India of Kipling's *Kim*, and "Judengasse," a poem that grieves over the vulnerability of a Jewish community in an Eastern European ghetto.

But in editing literary anthologies—the transforming influence of his *Anthology of Fantastic Literature* and his *Anthology of Detective Fiction* can hardly be underestimated—Borges drew on his wide-ranging interests in a focused way, and in the process shaped major achievements in Latin American literature, most recently the extravagant narratives of Roberto Bolaño, for whom Borges was a beloved antecedent.

Poems of the Night brings some of the thematic rigor of his anthologies to his own work. The first part, "A Poet Dreams," consists of poems Borges composed before he lost his sight.[10] These poems privilege the visual, particularly the crepuscular moments in which light turns to darkness. We see in this era the evolution of his metaphysical preoccupations, as when he alludes to Schopenhauer's suggestion that what we see may be a projection of our will, and that this insight is best appreciated in the twilight but placed in peril by dawn. We also experience his Argentine poems that evoke the observations and wanderings of a solitary explorer in an urban landscape in which there is scarcely another human presence, except for female presences in chaste trysts. These poems are bookish not only because they are philosophical meditations transformed into poems, but also because they evoke historical events that emphasize the violence of early Argentine nationhood.

The second part, "The Gift of Blindness," begins with the first poems Borges wrote after losing his sight in 1955, including "Poem of the Gifts," in which he conveys the irony of having been named director of the Argentine National Library when he could no longer read; this poem is enriched by a parallel he establishes with former librarian Paul Groussac, a writer he greatly admired. After writing it Borges learned he was not the second but the third national librarian in Argentina who had lost his sight, the first being the nineteenth-century novelist José Mármol. If the early poems featured a persona who wandered through his city, the wanderings of the second period are those of memory and recollection. Some of Borges's most daring gestures as a writer and reader of literature are to be found in these works. In "Conjectural Poem," for example, he imagines the fate of one of his ancestors killed by a gaucho militia in the nineteenth century, but at the same time he secretly completes an unfinished tale about a warrior in Dante's *Purgatorio*.[11] The poem is also an oblique image of a dilemma Borges often expressed about himself with irony, and that Edwin Williamson has explicated in *Borges: A Life*—the image of a man of letters born in Argentina who might have preferred to have lived a life of action.[12] Williamson has shown that when the poem was published it was intended and understood as an overt protest against Peronism in Argentina. In Borges's early commentaries on this poem he stressed its political significance, but in his later ones he recommends that his readers "note the influence of the dramatic monologues of Robert Browning."[13]

The third and final part, "Waiting for the Night," features poems inspired by his travels to feel, rather than to see, the places he had come to know through books, and dreams that brought him back to literature or to his native Argentina. It also features Borges's thoughts about his mortality, articulated with a certain pride, an abiding dignity, and, despite the presence of pain or angst, in a register that asserts a final serenity.

Like Paul Valéry, Juan Ramón Jiménez, and Alfonso Reyes, Borges worked on his poems endlessly. He continued to rewrite many of them whenever he edited new versions of his ever-changing collected poems—which he liked to call *Obra poética* (Poetic work)—or when he published new editions of his old books. Sometimes he would eliminate a poem altogether from a collection because he could not bear its flaws; other times he would remove one because he considered it a rough draft of a different poem with new inflections that would clash with other poems of an earlier period. He would even reconsider his originals when he collaborated on the translation of his poems into another language. In a dialogue with Norman Thomas di Giovanni—whose splendid *Selected Poems, 1923–1967* was the first major introduction to Borges's poetry in the English-speaking world—Borges recalls an instance when, in the translation process, he decided that his original Spanish ending could be improved. Instead of translating the original line into English, he opted for a different line, which he then translated back into Spanish in subsequent editions of his collected poems.[14] Another striking example of how Borges continued to edit his originals in the translation process is a poem originally titled "Resplandor" (Radiance) that Borges changed to "Ultimo resplandor" (Last radiance) in new editions and that di Giovanni cleverly translated as "Afterglow." Borges decided that no Spanish expression could match the English word, so in subsequent editions he kept the title in English for the Spanish poem. Even the French translation of the poem now uses the English word as its title.

Given Borges's proclivities as an editor of his work, it is inevitable that the earlier poems take on the qualities of Borges's maturing poetic vision, which downplayed his youthful enthusiasm for the shocking metaphor in search of a more direct mode of expression. In the 1930s, Borges repudiated his first three books of essays written in the 1920s because he could no longer abide their excessively stylized prose or identify with certain literary convictions he passionately defended as a young man: the ideas that literature is unambiguously autobiographical, that its significance is lost on those who ignore the circumstances of individual authors, and that it ought to express a nationality or a national character. He realized, however, that he did not need to repudiate his first books of poems, which could be edited to harmonize with his new vision and would anticipate later writings.

The first poem of this collection, "The Forging" (1922), anthologized here for the first time in an English translation, exemplifies Borges's editing habits. For anyone who knows that Borges was to lose his sight almost four decades later as a result of gradual degeneration, there is a prescient air when "The Forging"—an *ars poetica,* like many of his poems—opens with the image of a blind man who gropes with his hands for poetic lines that are to come. Borges reconsiders the earlier version when he changes "the weeping of the centuries" ("el llanto de los siglos") into the more subdued and realistic "the weeping of the evenings" ("el llanto de las tardes"), which Christopher Maurer elegantly renders as "the tears of evening." In a subsequent version of the poem, Borges eliminates a line—"y en lo callado se embravece un grito" ("and in the silence a scream takes heart")—that had appeared before the last couplet in order to offer a more serene, stoic ending to the poem. This is merely one instance of many revisions Borges attempted over the decades. We still need a critical edition of his verse, an edition that would trace Borges's creative process over the years as he edited and revised his poems. No such critical edition even exists for Borges's celebrated short stories, though there is, of course, a vertiginous number of scholarly and critical publications about his writings.

Poems of the Night follows the late Alexander Coleman's criterion in Penguin's *Selected Poems* (1999) by taking into account the final textual revisions made by Borges himself in his *Obras completas,* first published by Emecé in 1989.[15] But we included a version of "The Labyrinth" translated by John Updike in the 1960s (to honor Updike's pioneering role in promoting Latin American literature), and we restored Robert Fitzgerald's original translations of "Patio" and "Sepulchral Inscription" (which were skillfully adapted in the *Selected Poems* by Penny L. Fitzgerald to correspond to corrections Borges made after Fitzgerald's death). We wanted our reader to appreciate Fitzgerald's original choices as a translator as well as the process of revision; the later adaptations are included in the appendix on page 179, along with the 1921 version of "Insomnia," written in an avant-garde style Borges practiced as a youth but gave up when he published his first book of poems. The translators are listed at the beginning of this volume, and their initials appear at the end of each translation. Explanatory notes (including several by Borges himself) are included at the end of the book, as are all the sources of the poems, and an index of their titles in English and in Spanish.[16]

EFRAÍN KRISTAL

NOTES

1. Prologue to *Los conjurados* in *Selected Poems* (edited by Alexander Coleman), New York, Penguin, 1999, p. 469. Some of the quotations from the English will be slightly modified (note from the editor).

2. "Las dos maneras de traducir," *Textos Recobrados, 1919–1929*, p. 258. The essay is dated August 1, 1926. Borges modifies a text by Novalis and makes it his own. In the original, Novalis writes "Poesie der Nacht und Dämmerung," Novalis, Hermann Friedmann (ed.), *Werke. Dritter Teil. Fragmente I*, Berlin, Deutsches Verlagshaus, 1913, p. 213.

3. Cervera Salinas, Vicente, *La poesía de Jorge Luis Borges: historia de una eternidad*, Universidad de Murcia, 1992, p. 204.

4. Borges, Jorge Luis, "Blindness," in *Selected Non-Fictions* (edited by Eliot Weinberger), New York, Penguin, 1999, pp. 474–475.

5. Borges, "Nightmares," *Seven Nights*, Translated by Eliot Weinberger, New York, New Directions, 1984, pp. 32–33.

6. *Borges on Writing*, edited by Norman Thomas di Giovanni, Daniel Halpern, and Frank MacShane, Hopewell, N.J., The Echo Press, 1994, pp. 93–94.

7. Assiduous readers of Borges know that he often repeats or adapts sections of his poems in the other genres he practiced and vice versa. For a thoughtful analysis of Borges's practices of rewriting, see Michel Lafon, *Borges ou la réécriture*, Paris, Seuil, 1990.

8. Borges, *Selected Poems*, p. 147.

9. Borges's Whitmanian inflections are not cosmic, as in Octavio Paz, or earthy and political, as in Pablo Neruda.

10. Several poems in this section were eventually placed by Borges in books that were dated after he lost his sight, but they were originally published while he could still use his eyes to read and write. The following are the dates in which original versions of these poems were published: "Dreamtigers" (1934), "Insomnia" (1936), "The Cyclical Night" (1940), "Of Heaven and Hell" (1942), "Conjectural Poem" (1943), and "Museum" (1946).

11. Whereas the narrative of captain Buoconte of Montefeltro in Canto V of *Purgatorio* begins when his throat had been cut, Borges's poem ends when an "intimate knife" touches the throat of Narciso Laprida. See Kristal, Efraín, *Invisible Work: Borges and Translation*, Nashville, Vanderbilt University Press, 2002, pp. 170–172.

12. Williamson, Edwin. *Borges: A Life:* New York, Viking, 2004.

13. Borges, Prologue to *The Self and the Other*, p. 149.

14. *Borges on Writing*, p. 98.

15. Borges's collected poems went through several revisions from 1943 onward. John Updike's version of "The Labyrinth" was based on the 1967 edition of the *Obra poética*, Buenos Aires, Emecé.

16. Given that Penguin is publishing simultaneously a volume of Borges's sonnets, the only sonnet included in *Poems of the Night* is the first of a two-part poem, a diptych called "Two Versions of 'Knight, Death, and the Devil,'" and inspired by the famous Dürer etching. The sonnet is self-standing, but the second part of the poem invites readers to consider it in a new light.

Acknowledgments

I would like to express my gratitude to Suzanne Jill Levine for her editorial acumen, and to John Siciliano for his thoughtful input in determining the parameters of this volume. I am also very grateful to Alastair Reid, Stephen Kessler, Suzanne Jill Levine, Christopher Maurer, and John King for the new translations. Guillermo Guicci, Stephen Kessler, Kenneth Lincoln, John King, Trevor Merrill, Alfred Mac Adam, Jesús Torrecilla, and Christopher Maurer made thoughtful comments on parts of the manuscript. I thank Romy Sutherland for translating Borges's notes to his own poems. I would also like to acknowledge a UCLA Faculty Senate grant which secured the assistance of Román Luján for several practicalities.

EFRAÍN KRISTAL

Poems of the Night

I.

A POET DREAMS
(1922–1957)

FORJADURA

Como un ciego de manos precursoras
que apartan muros y vislumbran cielos,
lento de azoramiento voy palpando
por las noches hendidas
los versos venideros.
He de quemar la sombra abominable
en su límpida hoguera:
púrpura de palabras
sobre la espalda flagelada del tiempo.
He de encerrar el llanto de las tardes
en el duro diamante del poema.
Nada importa que el alma
ande sola y desnuda como el viento
si el universo de un glorioso beso
aún abarca mi vida.
Para ir sembrando versos
la noche es una tierra labrantía.

THE FORGING

Like the blind man whose hands are precursors
that push aside walls and glimpse heavens
slowly, flustered, I feel
in the crack of night
the verses that are to come.
I must burn the abominable darkness
in their limpid bonfire:
the purple of words
on the flagellated shoulder of time.
I must enclose the tears of evening
in the hard diamond of the poem.
No matter if the soul
walks naked and lonely as the wind
if the universe of a glorious kiss
still embraces my life.
The night is good fertile ground
for a sower of verses.

—C.M.

AMANECER

En la honda noche universal
que apenas contradicen los faroles
una racha perdida
ha ofendido las calles taciturnas
como presentimiento tembloroso
del amanecer horrible que ronda
los arrabales desmantelados del mundo.
Curioso de la sombra
y acobardado por la amenaza del alba
reviví la tremenda conjetura
de Schopenhauer y de Berkeley
que declara que el mundo
es una actividad de la mente,
un sueño de las almas,
sin base ni propósito ni volumen.
Y ya que las ideas
no son eternas como el mármol
sino inmortales como un bosque o un río,
la doctrina anterior
asumió otra forma en el alba
y la superstición de esa hora
cuando la luz como una enredadera
va a implicar las paredes de la sombra,
doblegó mi razón
y trazó el capricho siguiente:
Si están ajenas de sustancia las cosas
y si esta numerosa Buenos Aires
no es más que un sueño
que erigen en compartida magia las almas,
hay un instante
en que peligra desaforadamente su ser
y es el instante estremecido del alba,
cuando son pocos los que sueñan el mundo

BREAK OF DAY

In the deep night of the universe
scarcely contradicted by the streetlamps
a lost gust of wind
has offended the taciturn streets
like the trembling premonition
of the horrible dawn that prowls
the ruined suburbs of the world.
Curious about the shadows
and daunted by the threat of dawn,
I recalled the dreadful conjecture
of Schopenhauer and Berkeley
which declares that the world
is a mental activity,
a dream of souls,
without foundation, purpose, weight or shape.
And since ideas
are not eternal like marble
but immortal like a forest or a river,
the preceding doctrine
assumed another form as the sun rose,
and in the superstition of that hour
when light like a climbing vine
begins to implicate the shadowed walls,
my reason gave way
and sketched the following fancy:
If things are void of substance
and if this teeming Buenos Aires
is no more than a dream
made up by souls in a common act of magic,
there is an instant
when its existence is gravely endangered
and that is the shuddering instant of daybreak,
when those who are dreaming the world are few

y sólo algunos trasnochadores conservan,
cenicienta y apenas bosquejada,
la imagen de las calles
que definirán después con los otros.
¡Hora en que el sueño pertinaz de la vida
corre peligro de quebranto,
hora en que le sería fácil a Dios
matar del todo Su obra!

Pero de nuevo el mundo se ha salvado.
La luz discurre inventando sucios colores
y con algún remordimiento
de mi complicidad en el resurgimiento del día
solicito mi casa,
atónita y glacial en la luz blanca,
mientras un pájaro detiene el silencio
y la noche gastada
se ha quedado en los ojos de los ciegos.

and only the ones who have been up all night retain,
ashen and barely outlined,
the image of the streets
that later others will define.
The hour when the tenacious dream of life
runs the risk of being smashed to pieces,
the hour when it would be easy for God
to level His whole handiwork!

But again the world has been spared.
Light roams the streets inventing dirty colors
and with a certain remorse
for my complicity in the day's rebirth
I ask my house to exist,
amazed and icy in the white light,
as one bird halts the silence
and the spent night
stays on in the eyes of the blind.

—S.K.

UN PATIO

Con la tarde
se cansaron los dos o tres colores del patio.
La gran franqueza de la luna llena
ya no entusiasma su habitual firmamento.
Patio, cielo encauzado.
El patio es el declive
por el cual se derrama el cielo en la casa.
Serena,
la eternidad espera en la encrucijada de estrellas.
Grato es vivir en la amistad oscura
de un zaguán, de una parra y de un aljibe.

PATIO

With evening
the two or three colors of the patio grew weary.
The huge candor of the full moon
no longer enchants its usual firmament.
Patio: heaven's watercourse.
The patio is the slope
down which the sky flows into the house.
Serenely
eternity waits at the crossway of the stars.
It is lovely to live in the dark friendliness
of covered entrance way, arbor, and wellhead.

— R.F.

CALLE CON ALMACÉN ROSADO

Ya se le van los ojos a la noche en cada bocacalle
y es como una sequía husmeando lluvia.
Ya todos los caminos están cerca,
y hasta el camino del milagro.
El viento trae el alba entorpecida.
El alba es nuestro miedo de hacer cosas distintas y se nos
      viene encima.
Toda la santa noche he caminado
y su inquietud me deja
en esta calle que es cualquiera.
Aquí otra vez la seguridad de la llanura
en el horizonte
y el terreno baldío que se deshace en yuyos y alambres
y el almacén tan claro como la luna nueva de ayer tarde.
Es familiar como un recuerdo la esquina
con esos largos zócalos y la promesa de un patio.
¡Qué lindo atestiguarte, calle de siempre, ya que miraron tan
      pocas cosas mis días!
Ya la luz raya el aire.
Mis años recorrieron los caminos de la tierra y del agua
y sólo a vos te siento, calle dura y rosada.
Pienso si tus paredes concibieron la aurora,
almacén que en la punta de la noche eres claro.
Pienso y se me hace voz ante las casas
la confesión de mi pobreza:
no he mirado los ríos ni la mar ni la sierra,
pero intimó conmigo la luz de Buenos Aires
y yo forjo los versos de mi vida y mi muerte con esa luz de
      calle.
Calle grande y sufrida,
eres la única música de que sabe mi vida.

STREET WITH A PINK CORNER STORE

Gone into night are all the eyes from every intersection
and it's like a drought anticipating rain.
Now all roads are near,
even the road of miracles.
The wind brings with it a slow, befuddled dawn.
Dawn is our fear of doing different things and it comes
        over us.
All the blessed night I have been walking
and its restlessness has left me
on this street, which could be any street.
Here again the certainty of the plains
on the horizon
and the barren terrain that fades into weeds and wire
and the store as bright as last night's new moon.
The corner is familiar like a memory
with those spacious squares and the promise of a courtyard.
How lovely to attest to you, street of forever, since my own
        days have witnessed so few things!
Light draws streaks in the air.
My years have run down roads of earth and water
and you are all I feel, strong rosy street.
I think it is your walls that conceived sunrise,
store so bright in the depth of night.
I think, and the confession of my poverty
is given voice before these houses:
I have seen nothing of mountain ranges, rivers, or the sea,
but the light of Buenos Aires made itself my friend
and I shape the lines of my life and my death with that light
        of the street.
Big long-suffering street,
you are the only music my life has understood.

—S.K.

UNA DESPEDIDA

Tarde que socavó nuestro adiós.
Tarde acerada y deleitosa y monstruosa como un ángel
    oscuro.
Tarde cuando vivieron nuestros labios en la desnuda
    intimidad de los besos.
El tiempo inevitable se desbordaba
sobre el abrazo inútil.
Prodigábamos pasión juntamente, no para nosotros sino para
    la soledad ya inmediata.
Nos rechazó la luz; la noche había llegado con urgencia.
Fuimos hasta la verja en esa gravedad de la sombra que ya el
    lucero alivia.
Como quien vuelve de un perdido prado yo volví de tu
    abrazo.
Como quien vuelve de un país de espadas yo volví de tus
    lágrimas.
Tarde que dura vívida como un sueño
entre las otras tardes.
Después yo fui alcanzando y rebasando
noches y singladuras.

A LEAVETAKING

Evening that undermined our goodbye.
Steely, enchanted, monstrous evening like a dark angel.
Evening when our lips were alive in the naked intimacy of our
    kisses.
Time inevitably overflowed
and swamped our useless embrace.
Together we squandered our passion, not for ourselves but
    for the looming solitude.
Light rejected us; night came rushing down.
We went as far as the gate in that shadowy gravity now
    lightened by Venus.
As one returning from a lost meadow I returned from
    your arms.
As one returning from a country of swords I returned from
    your tears.
Evening that lasts vivid as a dream
among the other evenings.
Later I was reaching and exceeding
mere nights and days.

—s.k.

AFTERGLOW

Siempre es conmovedor el ocaso
por indigente o charro que sea,
pero más conmovedor todavía
es aquel brillo desesperado y final
que herrumbra la llanura
cuando el sol último se ha hundido.
Nos duele sostener esa luz tirante y distinta,
esa alucinación que impone al espacio
el unánime miedo de la sombra
y que cesa de golpe
cuando notamos su falsía,
como cesan los sueños
cuando sabemos que soñamos.

AFTERGLOW

The sunset is always moving
however gaudy or impoverished it is,
but even more moving
is that last, desperate glow
turning the plain rust colored
once the sun has at last gone down.
It hurts us to bear that strange, expanded light,
that hallucination infusing space
with unanimous fear of the dark,
which suddenly ends
when we realize it's an illusion,
as dreams end
when it dawns on us we're dreaming.

—S.K.

INSCRIPCION SEPULCRAL

Para el coronel Isidoro Suárez, mi bisabuelo

Dilató su valor sobre los Andes.
Contrastó montañas y ejércitos.
La audacia fue costumbre de su espada.
Impuso en Junín término venturoso a la lucha
y a las lanzas del Perú dio sangre española.
Escribió su censo de hazañas
en prosa rígida como los clarines belísonos.
Murió cercado de un destierro implacable.
Hoy es un poco de ceniza y de gloria.

JORGE LUIS BORGES

SEPULCHRAL INSCRIPTION

For Colonel Isidoro Suárez, my great-grandfather

His valor passed beyond the Andes.
He fought against mountains and armies.
Audacity was a habit with his sword.
At Junín he put a lucky end to the fight
and gave Spanish blood to Peruvian lances.
He wrote his roll of deeds
in prose inflexible as battlesinging trumpets.
He died walled in by implacable exile.
Now he is a handful of dust and glory.

— R.F.

REMORDIMIENTO POR
CUALQUIER MUERTE

Libre de la memoria y de la esperanza,
ilimitado, abstracto, casi futuro,
el muerto no es un muerto: es la muerte.
Como el Dios de los místicos,
de Quien deben negarse todos los predicados,
el muerto ubicuamente ajeno
no es sino la perdición y ausencia del mundo.
Todo se lo robamos,
no le dejamos ni un color ni una sílaba:
aquí está el patio que ya no comparten sus ojos,
allí la acera donde acechó su esperanza.
Hasta lo que pensamos podría estarlo pensando él también;
nos hemos repartido como ladrones
el caudal de las noches y de los días.

REMORSE FOR ANY
DEATH

Free of memory and hope,
unlimited, abstract, almost future,
the dead body is not somebody: It is death.
Like the God of the mystics,
whom they insist has no attributes,
the dead person is no one everywhere,
is nothing but the loss and absence of the world.
We rob it of everything,
we do not leave it one color, one syllable:
Here is the yard which its eyes no longer take up,
there is the sidewalk where it waylaid its hope.
It might even be thinking
what we are thinking.
We have divided among us, like thieves,
the treasure of nights and days.

—W.S.M.

INSCRIPCIÓN EN CUALQUIER SEPULCRO

No arriesgue el mármol temerario
gárrulas transgresiones al todopoder del olvido,
enumerando con prolijidad
el nombre, la opinión, los acontecimientos, la patria.
Tanto abalorio bien adjudicado está a la tiniebla
y el mármol no hable lo que callan los hombres.
Lo esencial de la vida fenecida
—la trémula esperanza,
el milagro implacable del dolor y el asombro del goce—
siempre perdurará.
Ciegamente reclama duración el alma arbitraria
cuando la tiene asegurada en vidas ajenas,
cuando tú mismo eres el espejo y la réplica
de quienes no alcanzaron tu tiempo
y otros serán (y son) tu inmortalidad en la tierra.

INSCRIPTION ON
ANY TOMB

Let not the rash marble risk
garrulous breaches of oblivion's omnipotence,
in many words recalling
name, renown, events, birthplace.
All those glass jewels are best left in the dark.
Let not the marble say what men do not.
The essentials of the dead man's life—
the trembling hope,
the implacable miracle of pain, the wonder of sensual
    delight—
will abide forever.
Blindly the uncertain soul asks to continue
when it is the lives of others that will make that happen,
as you yourself are the mirror and image
of those who did not live as long as you
and others will be (and are) your immortality on earth.

                                    —W.S.M.

EL GENERAL QUIROGA VA EN
COCHE AL MUERE

El madrejón desnudo ya sin una sed de agua
y una luna perdida en el frío del alba
y el campo muerto de hambre, pobre como una araña.

El coche se hamacaba rezongando la altura;
un galerón enfático, enorme, funerario.
Cuatro tapaos con pinta de muerte en la negrura
tironeaban seis miedos y un valor desvelado.

Junto a los postillones jineteaba un moreno.
Ir en coche a la muerte ¡qué cosa más oronda!
El general Quiroga quiso entrar en la sombra
llevando seis o siete degollados de escolta.

Esa cordobesada bochinchera y ladina
(meditaba Quiroga) ¿qué ha de poder con mi alma?
Aquí estoy afianzado y metido en la vida
como la estaca pampa bien metida en la pampa.

Yo, que he sobrevivido a millares de tardes
y cuyo nombre pone retemblor en las lanzas,
no he de soltar la vida por estos pedregales.
¿Muere acaso el pampero, se mueren las espadas?

JORGE LUIS BORGES

GENERAL QUIROGA RIDES TO HIS
DEATH IN A CARRIAGE

The watercourse dry of puddles, not a drop of water left,
and a moon gone out in the cold shiver of dawn,
and the countryside, poor as a church mouse, dying of
    hunger.

The coach swayed from side to side, creaking up the slope;
a great bulk of a coach, voluminous, funereal.
Four black horses with a tinge of death in their dark coats
were drawing six souls in terror and one wide awake
    and bold.

Alongside the postilions a black man was galloping.
To ride to your death in a carriage—what a splendid thing
    to do!
General Quiroga had in mind to approach the haunts of
    death
taking six or seven companions with slit throats as escort.

That gang from Córdoba, troublemakers, loudmouthed, shifty
(Quiroga was pondering), now what can they possibly do
    to me?
Here I am strong, secure, well set up in life
like the stake for tethering beasts to, driven deep in
    the pampa.

I, who have endured through thousands of afternoons
and whose name alone is enough to set the lances quivering,
will not lay down my life in this godforsaken wilderness.
Do the winds from the southwest die, by any chance? Do
    swords?

Pero al brillar el día sobre Barranca Yaco
hierros que no perdonan arreciaron sobre él;
la muerte, que es de todos, arreó con el riojano
y una de puñaladas lo mentó a Juan Manuel.

Ya muerto, ya de pie, ya inmortal, ya fantasma,
se presentó al infierno que Dios le había marcado,
y a sus órdenes iban, rotas y desangradas,
las ánimas en pena de hombres y de caballos.

But when the brightness of day shone on Barranca Yaco
weapons without mercy swooped in a rage upon him;
death, which is for all, rounded up the man from La Rioja
and more than one thrust of the dagger invoked Juan Manuel
    de Rosas.

Now dead, now on his feet, now immortal, now a ghost,
he reported to the Hell marked out for him by God,
and under his command there marched, broken and
    bloodless,
the souls in purgatory of his soldiers and his horses.

                                                    —A.R.

LA NOCHE QUE EN EL SUR
LO VELARON

A Letizia Álvarez de Toledo

Por el deceso de alguien
—misterio cuyo vacante nombre poseo y cuya realidad no
    abarcamos—
hay hasta el alba una casa abierta en el Sur,
una ignorada casa que no estoy destinado a rever,
pero que me espera esta noche
con desvelada luz en las altas horas del sueño,
demacrada de malas noches, distinta,
minuciosa de realidad.

A su vigilia gravitada en muerte camino
por las calles elementales como recuerdos,
por el tiempo abundante de la noche,
sin más oíble vida
que los vagos hombres de barrio junto al apagado almacén
y algún silbido solo en el mundo.

Lento el andar, en la posesión de la espera,
llego a la cuadra y a la casa y a la sincera puerta que busco
y me reciben hombres obligados a gravedad
que participaron de los años de mis mayores,
y nivelamos destinos en una pieza habilitada que mira
    al patio
—patio que está bajo el poder y en la integridad de la
    noche—
y decimos, porque la realidad es mayor, cosas indiferentes
y somos desganados y argentinos en el espejo
y el maté compartido mide horas vanas.

DEATHWATCH ON THE
SOUTHSIDE

To Letizia Álvarez de Toledo

By reason of someone's death—
a mystery whose empty name I know and whose reality is
     beyond us—
a house on the Southside stands open until dawn,
unfamiliar to me, and not to be seen again,
but waiting for me this night
with a wakeful light in the deep hours of sleep—
a house wasted away by bad nights and worn sharp
into a fineness of reality.

Toward its weighty deathwatch I make my way
through streets elemental as memories,
through time grown pure in plenitude of night,
with no more life to be heard
than neighborhood loiterers make near a corner store
and a whistler somewhere, lonely in the nightworld.

In my slow walk, in my expectancy,
I reach the block, the house, the plain door I am looking for,
where men constrained to gravity receive me,
men who had a part in my elders' years,
and we size up our destinies in a tidied room overlooking the
     yard,
a yard that is under the power and wholeness of night:
and we speak of indifferent things, reality here being greater,
and in the mirror we are Argentine, apathetic,
and the shared maté measures out useless hours.

Me conmueven las menudas sabidurías
que en todo fallecimiento se pierden
—hábito de unos libros, de una llave, de un cuerpo entre
   los otros—.
Yo sé que todo privilegio, aunque oscuro, es de linaje de
   milagro
y mucho lo es el de participar en esta vigilia,
reunida alrededor de lo que no se sabe: del Muerto,
reunida para acompañar y guardar su primera noche en la
   muerte.

(El velorio gasta las caras;
los ojos se nos están muriendo en lo alto como Jesús.)

¿Y el muerto, el increíble?
Su realidad está bajo las flores diferentes de él
y su mortal hospitalidad nos dará
un recuerdo más para el tiempo
y sentenciosas calles del Sur para merecerlas despacio
y brisa oscura sobre la frente que vuelve
y la noche que de la mayor congoja nos libra:
la prolijidad de lo real.

JORGE LUIS BORGES

I am touched by the frail wisdoms
lost in every man's death—
his habit of books, of a key, of one body among the others.
I know that every privilege, however obscure, is in the line of
    miracles,
and here is a great one: to take part in this vigil,
gathered around a being no one knows—the Dead Man,
gathered to keep him company and guard him, his first night
    in death.

(Faces grow haggard with watching:
our eyes are dying on the height like Jesus.)

And the dead man, the unbelievable?
His reality remains under the alien reality of flowers,
and his hospitality in death will give us
one memory more for time
and graven streets on the Southside, one by one to be
    savored,
and a dark breeze in my face as I walk home,
and night that frees us from that ordeal by weariness,
the daily round of the real.

                                                —R.F.

LA NOCHE DE SAN JUAN

El poniente implacable en esplendores
quebró a filo de espada las distancias.
Suave como un sauzal está la noche.
Rojos chisporrotean
los remolinos de las bruscas hogueras;
leña sacrificada
que se desangra en altas llamaradas,
bandera viva y ciega travesura.
La sombra es apacible como una lejanía;
hoy las calles recuerdan
que fueron campo un día.
Toda la santa noche la soledad rezando
su rosario de estrellas desparramadas.

ST. JOHN'S EVE

The setting sun, with implacable splendor,
parted the distances on its blade.
And night is here, tender as a willow.
Whorls of brusque bonfires
Splutter into red:
wood offered in sacrifice
bleeds into the high flames:
living flag, blind mischief.
The darkness is as gentle as someplace far away.
Today the streets remember
that they were fields one day.
And through the holy night,
Solitude says its rosary of far flung stars.

—C.M.

CASI JUICIO FINAL

Mi callejero *no hacer nada* vive y se suelta por la variedad de
  la noche.
La noche es una fiesta larga y sola.
En mi secreto corazón yo me justifico y ensalzo.
He atestiguado el mundo; he confesado la rareza del mundo.
He cantado lo eterno: la clara luna volvedora y las mejillas
  que apetece el amor.
He conmemorado con versos la ciudad que me ciñe
y los arrabales que se desgarran.
He dicho asombro donde otros dicen solamente costumbre.
Frente a la canción de los tibios, encendí mi voz en ponientes.
A los antepasados de mi sangre y a los antepasados de mis
    sueños
he exaltado y cantado.
He sido y soy.
He trabado en firmes palabras mi sentimiento
que pudo haberse disipado en ternura.
El recuerdo de una antigua vileza vuelve a mi corazón.
Como el caballo muerto que la marea inflige a la playa,
  vuelve a mi corazón.
Aún están a mi lado, sin embargo, las calles y la luna.
El agua sigue siendo grata en mi boca y el verso no me niega
  su música.
Siento el pavor de la belleza; ¿quién se atreverá a condenarme
  si esta gran luna de mi soledad me perdona?

ALMOST A LAST JUDGMENT

My doing nothing as I walk the streets lives on
and is released into the night's multiplicity.
The night is a long and lonely celebration.
In my secret heart I justify and glorify myself.
I have witnessed the world; I have confessed to the
    strangeness of the world.
I've sung the eternal: the bright returning moon and the faces
    craved by love.
I've recorded in poems the city that surrounds me
and the outlying neighborhoods tearing themselves apart.
I've said astonishment where others said only custom.
Faced with the song of the tepid, I ignited my voice in sunsets.
I've exalted and sung my blood's ancestors and the ancestors
of my dreams.
I have been and I am.
I've fixed my feelings into durable words
when they could have been spent on tenderness.
The memory of an old infamy returns to my heart.
Like a dead horse flung up on the beach by the tide, it returns
    to my heart.
And yet, the streets and the moon are still at my side.
Water keeps flowing freely in my mouth and poems don't
    deny me their music.
I feel the terror of beauty; who will dare condemn me when
    this great moon of my solitude forgives me?

—S.K.

DREAMTIGERS

En la infancia yo ejercí con fervor la adoración del tigre: no el
tigre overo de los camalotes del Paraná y de la confusión
amazónica, sino el tigre rayado, asiático, real, que sólo pueden
afrontar los hombres de guerra, sobre un castillo encima de un
elefante. Yo solía demorarme sin fin ante una de las jaulas en el
Zoológico; yo apreciaba las vastas enciclopedias y los libros de
historia natural, por el esplendor de sus tigres. (Todavía me
acuerdo de esas figuras: yo que no puedo recordar sin error la
frente o la sonrisa de una mujer.) Pasó la infancia, caducaron
los tigres y su pasión, pero todavía están en mis sueños. En esa
napa sumergida o caótica siguen prevaleciendo y así: Dormido,
me distrae un sueño cualquiera y de pronto sé que es un sueño.
Suelo pensar entonces: Éste es un sueño, una pura diversión de
mi voluntad, y ya que tengo un ilimitado poder, voy a causar
un tigre.

¡Oh, incompetencia! Nunca mis sueños saben engendrar la
apetecida fiera. Aparece el tigre, eso sí, pero disecado o endeble,
o con impuras variaciones de forma, o de un tamaño inadmis-
ible, o harto fugaz, o tirando a perro o a pájaro.

DREAMTIGERS

When I was a child, I came to worship tigers with a passion: not the yellow tigers of the Paraná River and the tangle of the Amazon but the striped tiger, the royal tiger of Asia, which can only be hunted by armed men from a fort on the back of an elephant. I would hang about endlessly in front of one of the cages in the Zoo; and I would prize the huge encyclopedias and books of natural history for the magnificence of their tigers. (I can still recall these illustrations vividly—I, who have trouble recalling the face or the smile of a woman.) My childhood passed and my passion for tigers faded, but they still appear in my dreams. In the unconscious or chaotic dimension, their presences persist, in the following way: While I am asleep, some dream or other disturbs me, and all at once I realize I am dreaming. At these moments, I tend to think to myself: This is a dream, simply an exercise of my will; and since my powers are limitless, I am going to dream up a tiger.

Utter incompetence! My dreaming is never able to conjure up the desired creature. A tiger appears, sure enough, but an enfeebled tiger, a stuffed tiger, imperfect of form, or the wrong size, or only fleetingly present, or looking something like a dog or a bird.

—A.R.

INSOMNIO

De fierro,
de encorvados tirantes de enorme fierro, tiene que ser
    la noche,
para que no la revienten y la desfonden
las muchas cosas que mis abarrotados ojos han visto,
las duras cosas que insoportablemente la pueblan.

Mi cuerpo ha fatigado los niveles, las temperaturas, las luces:
en vagones de largo ferrocarril,
en un banquete de hombres que se aborrecen,
en el filo mellado de los suburbios,
en una quinta calurosa de estatuas húmedas,
en la noche repleta donde abundan el caballo y el hombre.

El universo de esta noche tiene la vastedad
del olvido y la precisión de la fiebre.

En vano quiero distraerme del cuerpo
y del desvelo de un espejo incesante
que lo prodiga y que lo acecha
y de la casa que repite sus patios
y del mundo que sigue hasta un despedazado arrabal
de callejones donde el viento se cansa y de barro torpe.

En vano espero
las desintegraciones y los símbolos que preceden al sueño.

Sigue la historia universal:
los rumbos minuciosos de la muerte en las caries dentales,
la circulación de mi sangre y de los planetas.

(He odiado el agua crapulosa de un charco,
he aborrecido en el atardecer el canto del pájaro.)

JORGE LUIS BORGES

INSOMNIA

Of iron,
of bent struts of enormous iron the night must be made
to hold in all the things that have crowded my eyes
all the hard things that try unbearably
to burst her sides and bottom.

My body has roamed through levels, temperatures, lights:
in cars on long trains,
in a banquet of men who hate one another,
on the jagged edge of the suburbs,
in a warm villa with dripping statues,
in the full night where man and horse abound.

The universe of this night
is as vast as oblivion, as precise as fever.

In vain do I try to distract myself from my body
and the vigil of an incessant mirror
which multiplies it, lying in ambush,
and the house that repeats its courtyards
and the world that extends to the last broken-down
        neighborhood
of clumsy mud and alleys where the wind grows tired.

In vain do I await
the disintegration, the symbols that come before sleep.

Universal history goes on:
the tiny course of death through the cavities in our teeth,
the circulation of my blood and of the planets.

(I have hated the crapulous watter in a puddle,
the bird singing in the early hours.)

Las fatigadas leguas incesantes del suburbio del Sur,
leguas de pampa basurera y obscena, leguas de execración,
no se quieren ir del recuerdo.
Lotes anegadizos, ranchos en montón como perros, charcos
    de plata fétida:
soy el aborrecible centinela de esas colocaciones inmóviles.

Alambre, terraplenes, papeles muertos, sobras de Buenos
Aires.

Creo esta noche en la terrible inmortalidad:
ningún hombre ha muerto en el tiempo, ninguna mujer,
    ningún muerto,
porque esta inevitable realidad de fierro y de barro
tiene que atravesar la indiferencia de cuantos estén dormidos
    o muertos
—aunque se oculten en la corrupción y en los siglos—
y condenarlos a vigilia espantosa.

Toscas nubes color borra de vino infamarán el cielo;
amanecerá en mis párpados apretados.

Adrogué, 1936

The tired, incessant miles of this suburb in the South
the miles of garbage-strewn, obscene Pampa, the miles of
    execration
refuse to leave my memory.
Flooded lots, slums huddled like dogs, puddles of fetid silver:
I am the hateful watchman of those unmoving placements.

Wire, embankments, dead papers, scraps of Buenos Aires.

Tonight I believe in fearful immortality:
no man has died in time, no woman,
no dead person, for this inevitable reality of steel and mud
has to traverse the indifference of all who are dead or asleep
—though they hide in corruption and in the centuries—
and condemn them to a ghastly sleeplessness.

Rough clouds the color of wine lees will stain the sky.
and dawn will come to my tightly closed eyes.

—C.M.

LA NOCHE CÍCLICA

A Sylvina Bullrich

Lo supieron los arduos alumnos de Pitágoras:
Los astros y los hombres vuelven cíclicamente;
Los átomos fatales repetirán la urgente
Afrodita de oro, los tebanos, las ágoras.

En edades futuras oprimirá el centauro
Con el casco solípedo el pecho del lapita;
Cuando Roma sea polvo, gemirá en la infinita
Noche de su palacio fétido el minotauro.

Volverá toda noche de insomnio: minuciosa.
La mano que esto escribe renacerá del mismo
Vientre. Férreos ejércitos construirán el abismo.
(David Hume de Edimburgo dijo la misma cosa.)

No sé si volveremos en un ciclo segundo
Como vuelven las cifras de una fracción periódica;
Pero sé que una oscura rotación pitagórica
Noche a noche me deja en un lugar del mundo

Que es de los arrabales. Una esquina remota
Que puede ser del norte, del sur o del oeste,
Pero que tiene siempre una tapia celeste,
Una higuera sombría y una vereda rota.

Ahí está Buenos Aires. El tiempo que a los hombres
Trae el amor o el oro, a mí apenas me deja
Esta rosa apagada, esta vana madeja
De calles que repiten los pretéritos nombres

THE CYCLICAL NIGHT

To Sylvina Bullrich

They knew it, the fervent pupils of Pythagoras:
That stars and men revolve in a cycle,
That fateful atoms will bring back the vital
Gold Aphrodite, Thebans, and agoras.

In future epochs the centaur will oppress
With solid uncleft hoof the breast of the Lapith;
When Rome is dust the Minotaur will moan
Once more in the endless dark of its rank palace.

Every sleepless night will come back in minute
Detail. This writing hand will be born from the same
Womb, and bitter armies contrive their doom.
(Edinburgh's David Hume made this very point.)

I do not know if we will recur in a second
Cycle, like numbers in a periodic fraction;
But I know that a vague Pythagorean rotation
Night after night sets me down in the world

On the outskirts of this city. A remote street
Which might be either north or west or south,
But always with a blue-washed wall, the shade
Of a fig tree, and a sidewalk of broken concrete.

This, here, is Buenos Aires. Time, which brings
Either love or money to men, hands on to me
Only this withered rose, this empty tracery
Of streets with names recurring from the past

De mi sangre: Laprida, Cabrera, Soler, Suárez . . .
Nombres en que retumban (ya secretas) las dianas,
Las repúblicas, los caballos y las mañanas.
Las felices victorias, las muertes militares.

Las plazas agravadas por la noche sin dueño
Son los patios profundos de un árido palacio
Y las calles unánimes que engendran el espacio
Son corredores de vago miedo y de sueño.

Vuelve la noche cóncava que descifró Anaxágoras;
Vuelve a mi carne humana la eternidad constante
Y el recuerdo ¿el proyecto? de un poema incesante:
"Lo supieron los arduos alumnos de Pitágoras . . ."

In my blood: Laprida, Cabrera, Soler, Suárez . . .
Names in which secret bugle calls are sounding,
Invoking republics, cavalry, and mornings,
Joyful victories, men dying in action.

Squares weighed down by a night in no one's care
Are the vast patios of an empty palace,
And the single-minded streets creating space
Are corridors for sleep and nameless fear.

It returns, the hollow dark of Anaxagoras;
In my human flesh, eternity keeps recurring
And the memory, or plan, or an endless poem beginning:
"They knew it, the fervent pupils of Pythagoras . . ."

—A.R.

POEMA CONJETURAL

El doctor Francisco Laprida, asesinado el día
22 de setiembre de 1829 por los montoneros
de Aldao, piensa antes de morir:

Zumban las balas en la tarde última.
Hay viento y hay cenizas en el viento,
se dispersan el día y la batalla
deforme, y la victoria es de los otros.
Vencen los bárbaros, los gauchos vencen.
Yo, que estudié las leyes y los cánones,
yo, Francisco Narciso de Laprida,
cuya voz declaró la independencia
de estas crueles provincias, derrotado,
de sangre y de sudor manchado el rostro,
sin esperanza ni temor, perdido,
huyo hacia el Sur por arrabales últimos.
Como aquel capitán del Purgatorio
que, huyendo a pie y ensangrentando el llano,
fue cegado y tumbado por la muerte
donde un oscuro río pierde el nombre,
así habré de caer. Hoy es el término.
La noche lateral de los pantanos
me acecha y me demora. Oigo los cascos
de mi caliente muerte que me busca
con jinetes, con belfos y con lanzas.

Yo que anhelé ser otro, ser un hombre
de sentencias, de libros, de dictámenes,
a cielo abierto yaceré entre ciénagas;
pero me endiosa el pecho inexplicable
un júbilo secreto. Al fin me encuentro
con mi destino sudamericano.

CONJECTURAL POEM

Francisco Laprida, assassinated on the
22 of September of 1829 by the revolutionaries
from Aldao, reflects before his death:

Bullets whine on that last afternoon.
There is wind; and there is ash on the wind.
Now they subside, the day and the disorder
of battle, victory goes to the others,
to the barbarians. The gauchos win.
I, Francisco Narciso de Laprida,
who studied law and the civil canon,
whose voice proclaimed the independence
of these harsh provinces, am now defeated,
my face smeared with mingled blood and sweat,
lost, feeling neither hope nor fear,
in flight to the last outposts in the South.
Like that captain in the *Purgatorio*
who, fleeing on foot, leaving a bloodstained trail,
where some dark stream obliterates his name,
so must I fall. This day is the end.
The darkness spreading across the marshes
pursues me and pins me down. I hear the hooves
of my hot-breathing death hunting me down
with horsemen, whinnying, and lances.

I who dreamed of being another man,
well-read, a man of judgment and opinion,
will lie in a swamp under an open sky;
but a secret and inexplicable joy
makes my heart leap. At last I come face to face
with my destiny as a South American.
The complicated labyrinth of steps

A esta ruinosa tarde me llevaba
el laberinto múltiple de pasos
que mis días tejieron desde un día
de la niñez. Al fin he descubierto
la recóndita clave de mis años,
la suerte de Francisco de Laprida,
la letra que faltaba, la perfecta
forma que supo Dios desde el principio.
En el espejo de esta noche alcanzo
mi insospechado rostro eterno. El círculo
se va a cerra. Yo aguardo que así sea.

Pisan mis pies la sombra de las lanzas
que me buscan. Las befas de mi muerte,
los jinetes, las crines, los caballos,
se ciernen sobre mí . . . Ya el primer golpe,
ya el duro hierro que me raja el pecho,
el íntimo cuchillo en la garganta.

JORGE LUIS BORGES

that I have traced since one day in my childhood
led me to this disastrous afternoon.
At last I have discovered
the long-hidden secret of my life,
the destiny of Francisco de Laprida,
the missing letter, the key, the perfect form
known only to God from the beginning.
In the mirror of this night I come across
my eternal face, unknown to me. The circle
is about to close. I wait for it to happen.

My feet tread on the shadows of the lances
that point me out. The jeering at my death,
the riders, the tossing manes, the horses
loom over me . . . Now comes the first thrust,
now the harsh iron, ravaging my chest,
the knife, so intimate, opening my throat.

—A.R.

DEL INFIERNO Y DEL CIELO

El Infierno de Dios no necesita
el esplendor del fuego. Cuando el Juicio
Universal retumbe en las trompetas
y la tierra publique sus entrañas
y resurjan del polvo las naciones
para acatar la Boca inapelable,
los ojos no verán los nueve círculos
de la montaña inversa; ni la pálida
pradera de perennes asfódelos
donde la sombra del arquero sigue
la sombra de la corza, eternamente;
ni la loba de fuego que en el ínfimo
piso de los infiernos musulmanes
es anterior a Adán y a los castigos;
ni violentos metales, ni siquiera
la visible tiniebla de Juan Milton.
No oprimirá un odiado laberinto
de triple hierro y fuego doloroso
las atónitas almas de los réprobos.

Tampoco el fondo de los años guarda
un remoto jardín. Dios no requiere
para alegrar los méritos del justo,
orbes de luz, concéntricas teorías
de tronos, potestades, querubines,
ni el espejo ilusorio de la música
ni las profundidades de la rosa
ni el esplendor aciago de uno solo
de Sus tigres, ni la delicadeza
de un ocaso amarillo en el desierto
ni el antiguo, natal sabor del agua.
En Su misericordia no hay jardines
ni luz de una esperanza o de un recuerdo.

JORGE LUIS BORGES

OF HEAVEN AND HELL

The Inferno of God is not in need of
the splendor of fire. When, at the end of things,
Judgment Day resounds on the trumpets
and the earth opens and yields up its entrails
and nations reconstruct themselves from dust
to bow before the unappealable Judgment,
eyes then will not see the nine circles
of the inverted mountain, nor the pale
meadow of perennial asphodels
in which the shadow of the archer follows
the shadow of the deer, eternally,
nor the fiery ditch on the lowest level
of the infernos of the Muslim faith,
antedating Adam and the Fall,
nor the violence of metals, nor even
the almost visible blindness of Milton.
No fearful labyrinth of iron,
no doleful fires of suffering, will oppress
the awestruck spirits of the damned.

Nor does the far point of the years conceal
a secret garden. God does not require,
to celebrate the merits of the good life,
globes of light, concentric theories
of thrones and heavenly powers and cherubim,
nor the beguiling mirror that is music,
nor all the many meanings in a rose,
nor the fateful splendor of a single
one of his tigers, nor the subtleties
of a sunset turning gold in the desert,
nor the immemorial, natal taste of water.
In God's infinite care, there are no gardens,
no flash of hope, no glint of memory.

En el cristal de un sueño he vislumbrado
el Cielo y el Infierno prometidos:
cuando el Juicio retumbe en las trompetas
últimas y el planeta milenario
sea obliterado y bruscamente cesen
¡oh Tiempo! tus efímeras pirámides,
los colores y líneas del pasado
definirán en la tiniebla un rostro
durmiente, inmóvil, fiel, inalterable
(tal vez el de la amada, quizá el tuyo)
y la contemplación de ese inmediato
rostro incesante, intacto, incorruptible,
será para los réprobos, Infierno;
para los elegidos, Paraíso.

In the clear glass of a dream, I have glimpsed
the Heaven and Hell that lie in wait for us:
When Judgment Day sounds in the last trumpets
and planet and millennium both
disintegrate, and all at once, O Time,
all your ephemeral pyramids cease to be,
the colors and the lines that trace the past
will in the semidarkness form a face,
a sleeping face, faithful, still, unchangeable
(the face of the loved one, or, perhaps, your own)
and the sheer contemplation of that face—
never-changing, whole, beyond corruption—
will be, for the rejected, an Inferno,
and, for the elected, Paradise.

—A.R.

MUSEO

Cuarteta

Murieron otros, pero ello aconteció en el pasado,
Que es la estación (nadie lo ignora) más propicia a la muerte.
¿Es posible que yo, súbdito de Yaqub Almansur,
Muero como tuvieron que morir las rosas y Aristóteles?

—de Diván de Almotásim el Magrebí *(siglo xii)*

Límites

Hay una línea de Verlaine que no volveré a recordar,
Hay una calle próxima que está vedada a mis pasos,
Hay un espejo que me ha visto por última vez,
Hay una puerta que he cerrado hasta el fin del mundo
Entre los libros de mi biblioteca (estoy viéndolos)
Hay alguno que ya nunca abriré.
Este verano cumpliré cincuenta años;
La muerte me desgasta, incesante.

—de Inscripciones *(Montevideo, 1923), de Julio Platero Haedo*

MUSEUM

Quatrain

Other people died, but all that happened in the past,
the season (everyone knows) most propitious for death.
Can it be that I, a subject of Yaqub Almansur,
shall die as the roses have died, and Aristotle?

> —*from* The Divan of Almoqtádir the el-Maghrebi *(twelfth century)*
>
> —K.K.

Boundaries

There is a line by Verlaine that I will not remember again.
There is a street nearby that is off limits to my feet.
There is a mirror that has seen me for the last time.
There is a door I have closed until the end of the world.
Among the books in my library (I'm looking at them now)
    are some I will never open.
This summer I will be fifty years old.
Death is using me up, relentlessly.

> —*from* Inscriptions *(Montevideo, 1923) by Julio Platero Haedo*
>
> —K.K.

El poeta declara su nombradía

El círculo del cielo mide mi gloria,
Las bibliotecas del Oriente se disputan mis versos,
Los emires me buscan para llenarme de oro la boca,
Los ángeles ya saben de memoria mi último zéjel.
Mis instrumentos de trabajo son la humillación y la angustia;
Ojalá yo hubiera nacido muerto.

—*del* Divan de Abulcásim el Hadramí *(siglo xii)*

The Poet Proclaims His Renown

The span of heaven measures my glory.
Libraries in the East vie for my works.
Emirs seek me, to fill my mouth with gold.
The angels know my latest lyrics by heart.
The tools I work with are pain and humiliation.
Would that I had been born dead.

—*from* The Divan of Abulcasim el Hadrami *(twelfth century)*

—K.K.

JORGE LUIS BORGES

II.

THE GIFT OF BLINDNESS (1958–1977)

POEMA DE LOS DONES

Nadie rebaje a lágrima o reproche
Esta declaración de la maestría
De Dios, que con magnífica ironía
Me dio a la vez los libros y la noche.

De esta ciudad de libros hizo dueños
A unos ojos sin luz, que sólo pueden
Leer en las bibliotecas de los sueños
Los insensatos párrafos que ceden

Las albas a su afán. En vano el día
Les prodiga sus libros infinitos,
Arduos como los arduos manuscritos
Que perecieron en Alejandría.

De hambre y de sed (narra una historia griega)
Muere un rey entre fuentes y jardines;
Yo fatigo sin rumbo los confines
De esa alta y honda biblioteca ciega.

Enciclopedias, atlas, el Oriente
Y el Occidente, siglos, dinastías,
Símbolos, cosmos y cosmogonías
Brindan los muros, pero inútilmente.

Lento en mi sombra, la penumbra hueca
Exploro con el báculo indeciso,
Yo, que me figuraba el Paraíso
Bajo la especie de una biblioteca.

POEM OF THE GIFTS

No one should read self-pity or reproach
into this statement of the majesty
of God, who with such splendid irony
granted me books and blindness at one touch.

Care of this city of books he handed over
to sightless eyes, which now can do no more
than read in libraries of dream the poor
and senseless paragraphs that dawns deliver

to wishful scrutiny. In vain the day
squanders on these same eyes its infinite tomes,
as distant as the inaccessible volumes
that perished once in Alexandria.

From hunger and from thirst (in the Greek story),
a king lies dying among gardens and fountains.
Aimlessly, endlessly, I trace the confines,
high and profound, of this blind library.

Cultures of East and West, the entire atlas,
encyclopedias, centuries, dynasties,
symbols, the cosmos, and cosmogonies
are offered from the walls, all to no purpose.

In shadow, with a tentative stick, I try
the hollow twilight, slow and imprecise—
I, who had always thought of Paradise
in form and image as a library.

Algo, que ciertamente no se nombra
Con la palabra *azar,* rige estas cosas;
Otro ya recibió en otras borrosas
Tardes los muchos libros y la sombra.

Al errar por las lentas galerías
Suelo sentir con vago horror sagrado
Que soy el otro, el muerto, que habrá dado
Los mismos pasos en los mismos dias.

¿Cuál de los dos escribe este poema
De un yo plural y de una sola sombra?
¿Qué importa la palabra que me nombra
si es indiviso y uno el anatema?

Groussac o Borges, miro este querido
Mundo que se deforma y que se apaga
En una pálida ceniza vaga
Que se parece al sueño y al olvido.

Something, which certainly is not defined
by the word *fate,* arranges all these things;
another man was given, on other evenings
now gone, these many books. He too was blind.

Wandering through the gradual galleries,
I often feel with vague and holy dread
I am that other dead one, who attempted
the same uncertain steps on similar days.

Which of the two is setting down this poem—
a single sightless self, a plural I?
What can it matter, then, the name that names me,
given our curse is common and the same?

Groussac or Borges, now I look upon
this dear world losing shape, fading away
into a pale uncertain ashy-gray
that feels like sleep, or else oblivion.

—A.R.

LA LUNA

Cuenta la historia que en aquel pasado
Tiempo en que sucedieron tantas cosas
Reales, imaginarias y dudosas,
Un hombre concibió el desmesurado

Proyecto de cifrar el universo
En un libro y con ímpetu infinito
Erigió el alto y arduo manuscrito
Y limó y declamó el último verso.

Gracias iba a rendir a la fortuna
Cuando al alzar los ojos vio un bruñido
Disco en el aire y comprendió, aturdido,
Que se había olvidado de la luna.

La historia que he narrado, aunque fingida,
Bien puede figurar el maleficio
De cuantos ejercemos el oficio
De cambiar en palabras nuestra vida.

Siempre se pierde lo esencial. Es una
Ley de toda palabra sobre el numen.
No la sabrá eludir este resumen
De mi largo comercio con la luna.

No sé dónde la vi por vez primera,
Si en el cielo anterior de la doctrina
Del griego o en la tarde que declina
Sobre el patio del pozo y de la higuera.

THE MOON

The story goes that in those far-off times
when every sort of thing was taking place—
things real, imaginary, dubious things—
a man thought up a plan that would embrace

the universe entire in just one book.
Relentlessly spurred on by this vast notion,
he brought off the ambitious manuscript,
polishing the final verse with deep emotion.

All set to offer thanks to his good fortune,
he happened to look up and, none too soon,
beheld a glowing disk in the upper air,
the one thing he'd left out—the moon.

The story I have told, although made up,
could very well symbolize the plight
of those of us who cultivate the craft
of turning our lives into the words we write.

The essential thing is what we always miss.
From this law no one will be immune
nor will this account be an exception,
of my protracted dealings with the moon.

Where I saw it first I do not know,
whether in the other sky that, the Greeks tell,
preceded ours, or one fading afternoon
in the patio, above the fig-tree and the well.

Según se sabe, esta mudable vida
Puede, entre tantas cosas, ser muy bella
Y hubo así alguna tarde en que con ella
Te miramos, oh luna compartida.

Más que las lunas de las noches puedo
Recordar las del verso: la hechizada
Dragon moon que da horror a la balada
Y la luna sangrienta de Quevedo.

De otra luna de sangre y de escarlata
Habló Juan en su libro de feroces
Prodigios y de júbilos atroces;
Otras más claras lunas hay de plata.

Pitágoras con sangre (narra una
Tradición) escribía en un espejo
Y los hombres leían el reflejo
En aquel otro espejo que es la luna.

De hierro hay una selva donde mora
El alto lobo cuya extraña suerte
Es derribar la luna y darle muerte
Cuando enrojezca el mar la última aurora.

(Esto el Norte profético lo sabe
Y también que ese día los abiertos
Mares del mundo infestará la nave
Que se hace con las uñas de los muertos.)

Cuando, en Ginebra o Zürich, la fortuna
Quiso que yo también fuera poeta,
Me impuse, como todos, la secreta
Obligación de definir la luna.

As is well known, this changing life of ours
may incidentally seem ever so fair,
and so it was on evenings spent with her
when the moon was ours alone to share.

More than moons of the night, there come to mind
moons I have found in verse: the weirdly haunting
dragon moon that chills us in the ballad
and Quevedo's blood-stained moon, fully as daunting.

In the book he wrote full of all the wildest
wonders and atrocious jubilation,
John tells of a bloody scarlet moon.
There are other silver moons for consolation.

Pythagoras, an old tradition holds,
used to write his verse in blood on a mirror.
Men looked to its reflection in the moon's
hoping thus to make his meaning clearer.

In a certain ironclad wood is said to dwell
a giant wolf whose fate will be to slay
the moon, once he has knocked it from the sky
in the red dawning of the final day.

(This is well known throughout the prophetic North
as also that on that day, as all hope fails,
the seas of all the world will be infested
by a ship built solely out of dead men's nails.)

When in Geneva or Zurich the fates decreed
that I should be a poet, one of the few,
I set myself a secret obligation
to define the moon, as would-be poets do.

Con una suerte de estudiosa pena
Agotaba modestas variaciones.
Bajo el vivo temor de que Lugones
Ya hubiera usado el ámbar o la arena.

De lejano marfil, de humo, de fría
Nieve fueron las lunas que alumbraron
Versos que ciertamente no lograron
El arduo honor de la tipografía.

Pensaba que el poeta es aquel hombre
Que, como el rojo Adán del Paraíso,
Impone a cada cosa su preciso
Y verdadero y no sabido nombre.

Ariosto me enseñó que en la dudosa
Luna moran los sueños, lo inasible,
El tiempo que se pierde, lo posible
O lo imposible, que es la misma cosa.

De la Diana triforme Apolodoro
Me dejó divisar la sombra mágica;
Hugo me dio una hoz que era de oro,
Y un irlandés, su negra luna trágica.

Y, mientras yo sondeaba aquella mina
De las lunas de la mitología,
Ahí estaba, a la vuelta de la esquina,
La luna celestial de cada día.

Sé que entre todas las palabas, una
Hay para recordarla o figurarla.
El secreto, a mi ver, está en usarla
Con humildad. Es la palabra *luna*.

Working away with studious resolve,
I ran through my modest variations,
terrified that my moonstruck friend Lugones
would leave no sand or amber for *my* creations.

The moons that shed their silver on my lines
were moons of ivory, smokiness, or snow.
Needless to say, no typesetter ever saw
the faintest trace of their transcendent glow.

I was convinced that like the red-hot Adam
of Paradise, the poet alone may claim
to bestow on everything within his reach
its uniquely fitting, never-yet-heard-of name.

Ariosto holds that in the fickle moon
dwell dreams that slither through our fingers here,
all time that's lost, all things that might have been
or might not have—no difference, it would appear.

Apollodorus let me glimpse the threefold shape
Diana's magic shadow may assume.
Hugo gave me that reaper's golden sickle
and an Irishman his pitch-black tragic moon.

And as I dug down deep into that mine
of mythic moons, my still unquiet eye
happened to catch, shining around the corner,
the familiar nightly moon of our own sky.

To evoke our satellite there spring to mind
all those lunar clichés like *croon* and *June*.
The trick, however, is mastering the use
of a single modest word: that word is *moon*.

Ya no me atrevo a macular su pura
Aparición con una imagen vana;
La veo indescifrable y cotidiana
Y más allá de mi literatura.

Sé que la luna o la palabra *luna*
Es una letra que fue creada para
La compleja escritura de esa rara
Cosa que somos, numerosa y una.

Es uno de los símbolos que al hombre
Da el hado o el azar para que un día
De exaltación gloriosa o de agonía
Pueda escribir su verdadero nombre.

My daring fails. How can I continue
to thrust vain images in that pure face?
The moon, both unknowable and familiar,
disdains my claims to literary grace.

The moon I know or the letters of its name
were created as a puzzle or a pun
for the human need to underscore in writing
our untold strangenesses, many or one.

Include it then with symbols that fate or chance
bestow on humankind against the day—
sublimely glorious or plain agonic—
when at last we write its name the one true way.

—A.S.T.

ARTE POÉTICA

Mirar el río hecho de tiempo y agua
Y recordar que el tiempo es otro río,
Saber que nos perdemos como el río
Y que los rostros pasan como el agua.

Sentir que la vigilia es otro sueño
Que sueña no soñar y que la muerte
Que teme nuestra carne es esa muerte
De cada noche, que se llama sueño.

Ver en el día o en el año un símbolo
De los días del hombre y de sus años,
Convertir el ultraje de los años
En una música un rumor y un símbolo,

Ver en la muerte el sueño, en el ocaso
Un triste oro, tal es la poesía
Que es inmortal y pobre. La poesía
Vuelve como la aurora y el ocaso.

A veces en las tardes una cara
Nos mira desde el fondo de un espejo;
El arte debe ser como ese espejo
Que nos revela nuestra propia cara.

Cuentan que Ulises, harto de prodigios,
Lloró de amor al divisar su Itaca
Verde y humilde. El arte es esa Itaca
De verde eternidad, no de prodigios.

ARS POETICA

To look at the river made of time and water
And remember that time is another river,
To know that we are lost like the river
And that faces dissolve like water.

To be aware that waking dreams it is not asleep
While it is another dream, and that the death
That our flesh goes in fear of is that death
Which comes every night and is called sleep.

To see in the day or in the year a symbol
Of the days of man and of his years,
To transmute the outrage of the years
Into a music, a murmur of voices, and a symbol,

To see in death sleep, and in the sunset
A sad gold—such is poetry,
Which is immortal and poor. Poetry
Returns like the dawn and the sunset.

At times in the evenings a face
Looks at us out of the depths of a mirror;
Art should be like that mirror
Which reveals to us our own face.

They say that Ulysses, sated with marvels,
Wept tears of love at the sight of his Ithaca,
Green and humble. Art is that Ithaca
Of green eternity, not of marvels.

También es como el río interminable
Que pasa y queda y es cristal de un mismo
Heráclito inconstante, que es el mismo
Y es otro, como el río interminable.

It is also like the river with no end
That flows and remains and is the mirror of one same
Inconstant Heraclitus, who is the same
And is another, like the river with no end.

—w.s.m.

LOS ESPEJOS

Yo que sentí el horror de los espejos
No sólo ante el cristal impenetrable
Donde acaba y empieza, inhabitable,
un imposible espacio de reflejos

Sino ante el agua especular que imita
El otro azul en su profundo cielo
Que a veces raya el ilusorio vuelo
Del ave inversa o que un temblor agita

Y ante la superficie silenciosa
Del ébano sutil cuya tersura
Repite como un sueño la blancura
De un vago mármol o una vaga rosa,

Hoy, al cabo de tantos y perplejos
Años de errar bajo la varia luna,
Me pregunto qué azar de la fortuna
Hizo que yo temiera los espejos.

Espejos de metal, enmascarado
Espejo de caoba que en la bruma
De su rojo crepúsculo disfuma
Ese rostro que mira y es mirado,

Infinitos los veo, elementales
Ejecutores de un antiguo pacto,
Multiplicar el mundo como el acto
Generativo, insomnes y fatales.

JORGE LUIS BORGES

MIRRORS

I have been horrified before all mirrors
not just before the impenetrable glass,
the end and the beginning of that space,
inhabited by nothing but reflections,

but faced with specular water, mirroring
the other blue within its bottomless sky,
incised at times by the illusory flight
of inverted birds, or troubled by a ripple,

or face to face with the unspeaking surface
of ghostly ebony whose very hardness
reflects, as if within a dream, the whiteness
of spectral marble or a spectral rose.

Now, after so many troubling years
of wandering beneath the wavering moon,
I ask myself what accident of fortune
handed to me this terror of all mirrors—

mirrors of metal and the shrouded mirror
of sheer mahogany which in the twilight
of its uncertain red softens the face
that watches and in turn is watched by it.

I look on them as infinite, elemental
fulfillers of a very ancient pact
to multiply the world, as in the act
of generation, sleepless and dangerous.

Prolongan este vano mundo incierto
En su vertiginosa telaraña;
A veces en la tarde los empaña
El hálito de un hombre que no ha muerto.

Nos acecha el cristal. Si entre las cuatro
Paredes de la alcoba hay un espejo,
Ya no estoy solo. Hay otro. Hay el reflejo
Que arma en el alba un sigiloso teatro.

Todo acontece y nada se recuerda
En esos gabinetes cristalinos
Donde, como fantásticos rabinos,
Leemos los libros de derecha a izquierda.

Claudio, rey de una tarde, rey soñado,
No sintió que era un sueño hasta aquel día
En que un actor mimó su felonía
Con arte silencioso, en un tablado.

Que haya sueños es raro, que haya espejos,
Que el usual y gastado repertorio
De cada día incluya el ilusorio
Orbe profundo que urden los reflejos.

Dios (he dado en pensar) pone un empeño
En toda esa inasible arquitectura
Que edifica la luz con la tersura
Del cristal y la sombra con el sueño.

Dios ha creado las noches que se arman
De sueños y las formas del espejo
Para que el hombre sienta que es reflejo
Y vanidad. Por eso nos alarman.

They extenuate this vain and dubious world
within the web of their own vertigo.
Sometimes at evening they are clouded over
by someone's breath, someone who is not dead.

The glass is watching us. And if a mirror
hangs somewhere on the four walls of my room,
I am not alone. There's an other, a reflection
which in the dawn enacts its own dumb show.

Everything happens, nothing is remembered
in those dimensioned cabinets of glass
in which, like rabbis in fantastic stories,
we read the lines of text from right to left.

Claudius, king for an evening, king in a dream,
did not know he was a dream until that day
on which an actor mimed his felony
with silent artifice, in a tableau.

Strange, that there are dreams, that there are mirrors.
Strange that the ordinary, worn-out ways
of every day encompass the imagined
and endless universe woven by reflections.

God (I've begun to think) implants a promise
in all that insubstantial architecture
that makes light out of the impervious surface
of glass, and makes the shadow out of dreams.

God has created nights well-populated
with dreams, crowded with mirror images,
so that man may feel that he is nothing more
than vain reflection. That's what frightens us.

                                        —A.R.

LÍMITES

De estas calles que ahondan el poniente,
Una habrá (no sé cuál) que he recorrido
Ya por última vez, indiferente
Y sin adivinarlo, sometido

A Quién prefija omnipotentes normas
Y una secreta y rígida medida
A las sombras, los sueños y las formas
Que destejen y tejen esta vida.

Si para todo hay término y hay tasa
Y última vez y nunca más y olvido
¿Quién nos dirá de quién, en esta casa,
Sin saberlo, nos hemos despedido?

Tras el cristal ya gris la noche cesa
Y del alto de libros que una trunca
Sombra dilata por la vaga mesa,
Alguno habrá que no leeremos nunca.

Hay en el Sur más de un portón gastado
Con sus jarrones de mampostería
Y tunas, que a mi paso está vedado
Como si fuera una litografía.

Para siempre cerraste alguna puerta
Y hay un espejo que te aguarda en vano;
La encrucijada te parece abierta
Y la vigila, cuadrifronte, Jano.

LIMITS

Of all the streets that blur into the sunset,
there must be one (which, I am not sure)
that I by now have walked for the last time
without guessing it, the pawn of that Someone

who fixes in advance omnipotent laws,
sets up a secret and unwavering scale
for all the shadows, dreams, and forms
woven into the texture of this life.

If there is a limit to all things and a measure
and a last time and nothing more and forgetfulness,
who will tell us to whom in this house
we without knowing it have said farewell?

Through the dawning window night withdraws
and among the stacked books that throw
irregular shadows on the dim table,
there must be one which I will never read.

There is in the South more than one worn gate,
with its cement urns and planted cactus,
which is already forbidden to my entry,
inaccessible, as in a lithograph.

There is a door you have closed forever
and some mirror is expecting you in vain;
to you the crossroads seem wide open,
yet watching you, four-faced, is a Janus.

Hay, entre todas tus memorias, una
Que se ha perdido irreparablemente;
No te verán bajar a aquella fuente
Ni el blanco sol ni la amarilla luna.

No volverá tu voz a lo que el persa
Dijo en su lengua de aves y de rosas,
Cuando al ocaso, ante la luz dispersa,
Quieras decir inolvidables cosas.

¿Y el incesante Ródano y el lago,
Todo ese ayer sobre el cual hoy me inclino?
Tan perdido estará como Cartago
Que con fuego y con sal borró el latino.

Creo en el alba oír un atareado
Rumor de multitudes que se alejan;
Son lo que me ha querido y olvidado;
Espacio y tiempo y Borges ya me dejan.

There is among all your memories one
which has now been lost beyond recall.
You will not be seen going down to that fountain,
neither by white sun nor by yellow moon.

You will never recapture what the Persian
said in his language woven with birds and roses,
when, in the sunset, before the light disperses,
you wish to give words to unforgettable things.

And the steadily flowing Rhone and the lake,
all that vast yesterday over which today I bend?
They will be as lost as Carthage,
scourged by the Romans with fire and salt.

At dawn I seem to hear the turbulent
murmur of crowds milling and fading away;
they are all I have been loved by, forgotten by;
space, time, and Borges now are leaving me.

— A.R.

EL GOLEM

Si (como el griego afirma en el Cratilo)
El nombre es arquetipo de la cosa,
En las letras de *rosa* está la rosa
Y todo el Nilo en la palabra *Nilo*.

Y, hecho de consonantes y vocales,
Habrá un terrible Nombre, que la esencia
Cifre de Dios y que la Omnipotencia
Guarde en letras y sílabas cabales.

Adán y las estrellas lo supieron
En el Jardín. La herrumbre del pecado
(Dicen los cabalistas) lo ha borrado
Y las generaciones lo perdieron.

Los artificios y el candor del hombre
No tienen fin. Sabemos que hubo un día
En que el pueblo de Dios buscaba el Nombre
En las vigilias de la judería.

No a la manera de otras que una vaga
Sombra insinúan en la vaga historia,
Aún está verde y viva la memoria
De Judá León, que era rabino en Praga.

Sediento de saber lo que Dios sabe,
Judá León se dio a permutaciones
De letras y a complejas variaciones
Y al fin pronunció el Nombre que es la Clave,

THE GOLEM

If, as the Greek maintains in the *Cratylus*,
a name is the archetype of a thing,
the rose is in the letters that spell rose
and the Nile entire resounds in its name's ring.

So, composed of consonants and vowels,
there must exist one awe-inspiring word
that God inheres in—that, when spoken, holds
Almightiness in syllables unslurred.

Adam knew it in the Garden, so did the stars.
The rusty work of sin, so the cabbalists say,
obliterated it completely;
no generation has found it to this day.

The cunning and naïveté of men
are limitless. We know there came a time
when God's people, searching for the Name,
toiled in the ghetto, matching rhyme to rhyme.

One memory stands out, unlike the rest—
dim shapes always fading from time's dim log.
Still fresh and green the memory persists
of Judah León, a rabbi once in Prague.

Thirsty to know things only known to God,
Judah León shuffled letters endlessly,
trying them out in subtle combinations
till at last he uttered the Name that is the Key,

La Puerta, el Eco, el Huésped y el Palacio,
Sobre un muñeco que con torpes manos
Labró, para enseñarle los arcanos
De las Letras, del Tiempo y del Espacio.

El simulacro alzó los soñolientos
Párpados y vio formas y colores
Que no entendió, perdidos en rumores
Y ensayó temerosos movimientos.

Gradualmente se vio (como nosotros)
Aprisionado en esta red sonora
De Antes, Después, Ayer, Mientras, Ahora,
Derecha, Izquierda, Yo, Tú, Aquellos, Otros.

(El cabalista que ofició de numen
A la vasta criatura apodó Golem;
Estas verdades las refiere Scholem
En un docto lugar de su volumen.)

El rabí le explicaba el universo
"Esto es mi pie; esto el tuyo; esto la soga."
Y logró, al cabo de años, que el perverso
Barriera bien o mal la sinagoga.

Tal vez hubo un error en la grafía
O en la articulación del Sacro Nombre;
A pesar de tan alta hechicería,
No aprendió a hablar el aprendiz de hombre.

Sus ojos, menos de hombre que de perro
Y harto menos de perro que de cosa,
Seguían al rabí por la dudosa
Penumbra de las piezas del encierro.

the Gate, the Echo, the Landlord, and the Mansion,
over a dummy which, with fingers wanting grace,
he fashioned, thinking to teach it the arcana
of Words and Letters and of Time and Space.

The simulacrum lifted its drowsy lids
and, much bewildered, took in color and shape
in a floating world of sounds. Following this,
it hesitantly took a timid step.

Little by little it found itself, like us,
caught in the reverberating weft
of After, Before, Yesterday, Meanwhile, Now,
You, Me, Those, the Others, Right and Left.

That cabbalist who played at being God
gave his spacey offspring the nickname Golem.
(In a learned passage of his volume,
these truths have been conveyed to us by Scholem.)

To it the rabbi would explain the universe—
"This is my foot, this yours, this is a clog"—
year in, year out, until the spiteful thing
rewarded him by sweeping the synagogue.

Perhaps the sacred name had been misspelled
or in its uttering been jumbled or too weak.
The potent sorcery never took effect:
man's apprentice never learned to speak.

Its eyes, less human than doglike in their look,
and even less a dog's than eyes of a thing,
would follow every move the rabbi made
about a confinement always gloomy and dim.

Algo anormal y tosco hubo en el Golem,
Ya que a su paso el gato del rabino
Se escondía. (Ese gato no está en Scholem
Pero, a través del tiempo, lo adivino.)

Elevando a su Dios manos filiales,
Las devociones de su Dios copiaba
O, estúpido y sonriente, se ahuecaba
En cóncavas zalemas orientales.

El rabí lo miraba con ternura
Y con algún horror. *¿Cómo (se dijo)*
Pude engendrar este penoso hijo
Y la inacción dejé, que es la cordura?

¿Por qué di en agregar a la infinita
Serie un símbolo más? ¿Por qué a la vana
Madeja que en lo eterno se devana,
Di otra causa, otro efecto y otra cuita?

En la hora de angustia y de luz vaga,
En su Golem los ojos detenía.
¿Quién nos dirá las cosas que sentia
Dios, al mirar a su rabino en Praga?

Something coarse and abnormal was in the Golem,
for the rabbi's cat, as soon as it moved about,
would run off and hide. (There's no cat in Scholem
but across the gulf of time I make one out.)

Lifting up to its God its filial hands,
it aped its master's devotions—even the least—
or, with a stupid smile, would bend far over
in concave salaams the way men do in the East.

The rabbi watched it fondly and not a little
alarmed as he wondered: "How could I bring
such a sorry creature into this world
and give up my leisure, surely the wisest thing?

What made me supplement the endless series
of symbols with one more? Why add in vain
to the knotty skein always unraveling
another cause and effect, with not one gain?"

In his hour of anguish and uncertain light,
upon his Golem his eyes would come to rest.
Who is to say what God must have been feeling,
Looking down and seeing His rabbi so distressed?

                                                            —A.S.T.

ALGUIEN

Un hombre trabajado por el tiempo,
un hombre que ni siquiera espera la muerte
(las pruebas de la muerte son estadísticas
y nadie hay que no corra el albur
de ser el primer inmortal),
un hombre que ha aprendido a agradecer
las modestas limosnas de los días:
el sueño, la rutina, el sabor del agua,
una no sospechada etimología,
un verso latino o sajón,
la memoria de una mujer que lo ha abandonado
hace ya tantos años
que hoy puede recordarla sin amargura,
un hombre que no ignora que el presente
ya es el porvenir y el olvido,
un hombre que ha sido desleal
y con el que fueron desleales,
puede sentir de pronto, al cruzar la calle,
una misteriosa felicidad
que no viene del lado de la esperanza
sino de una antigua inocencia,
de su propia raíz o de un dios disperso.

Sabe que no debe mirarla de cerca,
porque hay razones más terribles que tigres
que le demostrarán su obligación
de ser un desdichado,
pero humildemente recibe
esa felicidad, esa ráfaga.

JORGE LUIS BORGES

SOMEONE

A man worn down by time,
a man who does not even expect death
(the proofs of death are statistics
and everyone runs the risk
of being the first immortal),
a man who has learned to express thanks
for the days' modest alms:
sleep, routine, the taste of water,
an unsuspected etymology,
a Latin or Saxon verse,
the memory of a woman who left him
thirty years ago now
whom he can call to mind without bitterness,
a man who is aware that the present
is both future and oblivion,
a man who has betrayed
and has been betrayed,
may feel suddenly, when crossing the street,
a mysterious happiness
not coming from the side of hope
but from an ancient innocence,
from his own root or from some diffused god.

He knows better than to look at it closely,
for there are reasons more terrible than tigers
which will prove to him
that wretchedness is his duty,
but he accepts humbly
this felicity, this glimmer.

Quizá en la muerte para siempre seremos,
cuando el polvo sea polvo,
esa indescifrable raíz,
de la cual para siempre crecerá,
ecuánime o atroz,
nuestro solitario cielo o infierno.

Perhaps in death when the dust
is dust, we will be forever
this undecipherable root,
from which will grow forever,
serene or horrible,
our solitary heaven or hell.

—W.S.M.

¿DÓNDE SE HABRÁN IDO?

Según su costumbre, el sol
Brilla y muere, muere y brilla
Y en el patio, como ayer,
Hay una luna amarilla,
Pero el tiempo, que no ceja,
Todas las cosas mancilla—
Se acabaron los valientes
Y no han dejado semilla.

¿Dónde están los que salieron
A libertar las naciones
O afrontaron en el Sur
Las lanzas de los malones?
¿Dónde están los que a la guerra
Marchaban en batallones?
¿Dónde están los que morían
En otras revoluciones?

—No se aflija. En la memoria
De los tiempos venideros
También nosotros seremos
Los tauras y los primeros.

El ruin será generoso
Y el flojo será valiente:
No hay cosa como la muerte
Para mejorar la gente.

JORGE LUIS BORGES

WHERE CAN THEY HAVE GONE?

In keeping with its custom, the sun
Sparkles and wanes, sparkles and wanes
And in the patio, like the night
Before, a yellow moon obtains,
But subtle time, which won't relent,
Affects all matter with its stains—
The valiant have disappeared
And left no hope. No seed remains.

Where are the ones who took their leave
To liberate the struggling nations
Or in the South defied the lances
Of Indian raids and conflagrations?
Where are those who marched off to war
In regiments, in strict formations?
Where are they now, who gave their deaths
To other worthy revolutions?

—Do not despair. In memory
Of uninaugurated years
We too will be uplifted as
Protectors and as pioneers.

The pettiest will be generous
And the most craven will be brave:
Nothing improves a reputation
Like confinement to a grave.

¿Dónde está la valerosa
Chusma que pisó esta tierra,
La que doblar no pudieron
Perra vida y muerte perra,
Los que en el duro arrabal
Vivieron como en la guerra,
Los Muraña por el Norte
Y por el Sur los Iberra?

¿Qué fue de tanto animoso?
¿Qué fue de tanto bizarro?
A todos los gastó el tiempo,
A todos los tapa el barro.
Juan Muraña se olvidó
Del cadenero y del carro
Y ya no sé si Moreira
Murió en Lobos o en Navarro.

—No se aflija. En la memoria . . .

What has become of the intrepid
Masses who stepped upon this earth,
Who would not be encumbered by
Death's bitter end, life's bitter berth,
The ones who lived as though at war
At the hard edge, in comfort's dearth,
The poor Iberras of the South
And the Murañas of the North?

What has become of so much spirit?
What has become of so many heroes?
All lie beneath the mud and clay,
All spent by infinite tomorrows.
Juan Muraña forgot about
The shackle-bearer and the barrow
And I no longer know if Moreira
Died in Lobos or Navarro.

—Do not despair. In memory . . .

—E.M.

HERÁCLITO

El segundo crepúsculo.
La noche que se ahonda en el sueño.
La purificación y el olvido.
El primer crepúsculo.
La mañana que ha sido el alba.
El día que fue la mañana.
El día numeroso que será la tarde gastada.
El segundo crepúsculo.
Ese otro hábito del tiempo, la noche.
La purificación y el olvido.
El primer crepúsculo . . .
El alba sigilosa y en el alba
la zozobra del griego.
¿Qué trama es ésta
del será, del es y del fue?
¿Qué río es éste
por el cual corre el Ganges?
¿Qué río es éste cuya fuente es inconcebible?
¿Qué río es éste
que arrastra mitologías y espadas?
Es inútil que duerma.
Corre en el sueño, en el desierto, en un sótano.
El río me arrebata y soy ese río.
De una materia deleznable fui hecho, de misterioso tiempo.
Acaso el manantial está en mí.
Acaso de mi sombra
surgen, fatales e ilusorios, los días.

HERACLITUS

The second twilight.
The night sinking into sleep.
Purification and oblivion.
The first twilight.
The morning that was dawn.
The day that was morning.
The day of a thousand things that will be the spent afternoon.
The second twilight.
That other habit of time, the night.
Purification and oblivion.
The first twilight . . .
Secretive dawn and at dawn
the Greek's anxiety.
What scheme is this
of it will be, it is and it was?
What river is this
where the Ganges flows?
What river is this whose source is inconceivable?
What river is this
bearing along mythologies and swords?
It would be useless for it to sleep.
It flows through sleep, through the desert, through a
    basement.
The river carries me off and I am that river.
I was made of wretched stuff, mysterious time.
Perhaps the source is inside me.
Perhaps the fatal and illusory days
spring from my shadow.

—S.K.

EL LABERINTO

Zeus no podría desatar las redes
De piedra que me cercan. He olvidado
Los hombres que antes fui; sigo el odiado
Camino de monótonas paredes
Que es mi destino. Rectas galerías
Que se curvan en círculos secretos
Al cabo de los años. Parapetos
Que ha agrietado la usura de los días.
En el pálido polvo he descifrado
Rastros que temo. El aire me ha traído
En las cóncavas tardes un bramido
O el eco de un bramido desolado.
Sé que en la sombra hay Otro, cuya suerte
Es fatigar las largas soledades
Que tejen y destejen este Hades
Y ansiar mi sangre y devorar mi muerte.
Nos buscamos los dos. Ojalá fuera
Este el último día de la espera.

THE LABYRINTH

Zeus, Zeus himself could not undo these nets
Of stone encircling me. My mind forgets
The persons I have been along the way,
The hated way of monotonous walls,
Which is my fate. The galleries seem straight
But curve furtively, forming secret circles
At the terminus of years; and the parapets
Have been worn smooth by the passage of days.
Here, in the tepid alabaster dust,
Are tracks that frighten me. The hollow air
Of evening sometimes brings a bellowing,
Or the echo, desolate, of bellowing.
I know that hidden in the shadows there
Lurks another, whose task is to exhaust
The loneliness that braids and weaves this hell,
To crave my blood, and to fatten on my death.
We seek each other. Oh, if only this
Were the last day of our antithesis!

—J.U.

DOS VERSIONES DE "RITTER, TOD UND TEUFEL"

I

Bajo el yelmo quimérico el severo
Perfil es cruel como la cruel espada
Que aguarda. Por la selva despojada
Cabalga imperturbable el caballero.
Torpe y furtiva, la caterva obscena
Lo ha cercado: el Demonio de serviles
Ojos, los laberínticos reptiles
Y el blanco anciano del reloj de arena.
Caballero de hierro, quien te mira
Sabe que en ti no mora la mentira
Ni el pálido temor. Tu dura suerte
Es mandar y ultrajar. Eres valiente
Y no serás indigno ciertamente,
Alemán, del Demonio y de la Muerte.

II

Los caminos son dos. El de aquel hombre
De hierro y de soberbia, y que cabalga,
Firme en su fe, por la dudosa selva
Del mundo, entre las befas y la danza
Inmóvil del Demonio y de la Muerte,
Y el otro, el breve, el mío. ¿En qué borrada
Noche o mañana antigua descubrieron
Mis ojos la fantástica epopeya,
El perdurable sueño de Durero,
El héroe y la caterva de sus sombras
Que me buscan, me acechan y me encuentran:
A mí, no al paladín, exhorta el blanco
Anciano coronado de sinuosas

TWO VERSIONS OF "KNIGHT, DEATH, AND THE DEVIL"

I

Under the unreal helmet the severe
Profile is cruel like the cruel sword
Waiting, poised. Through the stripped forest
Rides the horseman unperturbed.
Clumsily, furtively, the obscene mob
Closes in on him: the Devil with servile
Eyes, the labyrinthine reptiles
And the ashen old man with the hourglass.
Iron rider, whoever looks at you
Knows that in you neither the lie
Nor pale fear dwells. Your hard fate
Is to command and offend. You are brave
And you are certainly not unworthy,
German, of the Devil and of Death.

II

There are two roads. That of the man
Of iron and arrogance, who rides,
Firm in his faith, through the doubtful woods
Of the world, between the taunts and the rigid
Dance of the Devil with Death,
And the other, the short one, mine. In what vanished
Long-ago night or morning did my eyes
Discover the fantastic epic,
The enduring dream of Dürer,
The hero and the mob with all its shadows
Searching me out, and catching me in ambush?
It is me, and not the paladin, whom the hoary
Old man crowned with sinuous snakes

Serpientes. La clepsidra sucesiva
Mide mi tiempo, no su eterno ahora.
Yo seré la ceniza y la tiniebla;
Yo, que partí después, habré alcanzado
Mi término mortal; tú, que no eres,
Tú, caballero de la recta espada
Y de la selva rígida, tu paso
Proseguirás mientras los hombres duren.
Imperturbable, imaginario, eterno.

Is warning. The future's water clock
Measures my time, not his eternal now.
I am the one who will be ashes and darkness;
I, who set out later, will have reached
My mortal destination; you, who do not exist,
You, rider of the raised sword
And the rigid woods, your pace
Will keep on going as long as there are men.
Composed, imaginary, eternal.

—S.K.

ELOGIO DE LA SOMBRA

La vejez (tal es el nombre que los otros le dan)
puede ser el tiempo de nuestra dicha.
El animal ha muerto o casi ha muerto.
Quedan el hombre y su alma.
Vivo entre formas luminosas y vagas
que no son aún la tiniebla.
Buenos Aires,
que antes se desgarraba en arrabales
hacia la llanura incesante,
ha vuelto a ser la Recoleta, el Retiro,
las borrosas calles del Once
y las precarias casas viejas
que aún llamamos el Sur.
Siempre en mi vida fueron demasiadas las cosas;
Demócrito de Abdera se arrancó los ojos para pensar;
el tiempo ha sido mi Demócrito.
Esta penumbra es lenta y no duele;
fluye por un manso declive
y se parece a la eternidad.
Mis amigos no tienen cara,
las mujeres son lo que fueron hace ya tantos años,
las esquinas pueden ser otras,
no hay letras en las páginas de los libros.
Todo esto debería atemorizarme,
pero es una dulzura, un regreso.
De las generaciones de los textos que hay en la tierra
sólo habré leído unos pocos,
los que sigo leyendo en la memoria,
leyendo y transformando.
Del Sur, del Este, del Oeste, del Norte,
convergen los caminos que me han traído
a mi secreto centro.
Esos caminos fueron ecos y pasos,

IN PRAISE OF DARKNESS

Old age (the name that others give it)
can be the time of our greatest bliss.
The animal has died or almost died.
The man and his spirit remain.
I live among vague, luminous shapes
that are not darkness yet.
Buenos Aires,
whose edges disintegrated
into the endless plain,
has gone back to being the Recoleta, the Retiro,
the nondescript streets of the Once,
and the rickety old houses
we still call the South.
In my life there were always too many things.
Democritus of Abdera plucked out his eyes in order to think:
Time has been my Democritus.
This penumbra is slow and does not pain me;
it flows down a gentle slope,
resembling eternity.
My friends have no faces,
women are what they were so many years ago,
these corners could be other corners,
there are no letters on the pages of books.
All this should frighten me,
but it is a sweetness, a return.
Of the generations of texts on earth
I will have read only a few—
the ones that I keep reading in my memory,
reading and transforming.
From South, East, West, and North
the paths converge that have led me
to my secret center.
Those paths were echoes and footsteps,

mujeres, hombres, agonías, resurrecciones,
días y noches,
entresueños y sueños,
cada ínfimo instante del ayer
y de los ayeres del mundo,
la firme espada del danés y la luna del persa,
los actos de los muertos,
el compartido amor, las palabras,
Emerson y la nieve y tantas cosas.
Ahora puedo olvidarlas. Llego a mi centro,
a mi álgebra y mi clave,
a mi espejo.
Pronto sabré quién soy.

women, men, death-throes, resurrections,
days and nights,
dreams and half-wakeful dreams,
every inmost moment of yesterday
and all the yesterdays of the world,
the Dane's staunch sword and the Persian's moon,
the acts of the dead,
shared love, and words,
Emerson and snow, so many things.
Now I can forget them. I reach my center,
my algebra and my key,
my mirror.
Soon I will know who I am.

—H.R.

EL ORO DE LOS TIGRES

Hasta la hora del ocaso amarillo
Cuántas veces habré mirado
Al poderoso tigre de Bengala
Ir y venir por el predestinado camino
Detrás de los barrotes de hierro,
Sin sospechar que eran su cárcel.
Después vendrían otros tigres,
El tigre de fuego de Blake;
Después vendrían otros oros,
El metal amoroso que era Zeus,
El anillo que cada nueve noches
Engendra nueve anillos y éstos, nueve,
Y no hay un fin.
Con los años fueron dejándome
Los otros hermosos colores
Y ahora sólo me quedan
La vaga luz, la inextricable sombra
Y el oro del principio.
Oh ponientes, oh tigres, oh fulgores
Del mito y de la épica,
Oh un oro más precioso, tu cabello
Que ansían estas manos.

East Lansing, 1972

THE GOLD OF THE TIGERS

Up to the moment of the yellow sunset,
how many times will I have cast my eyes on
the sinewy-bodied tiger of Bengal
to-ing and fro-ing on its paced-out path
behind the labyrinthine iron bars,
never suspecting them to be a prison.
Afterwards, other tigers will appear:
the blazing tiger of Blake, burning bright;
and after that will come the other golds—
the amorous gold shower disguising Zeus,
the gold ring which, on every ninth night,
gives light to nine rings more, and these, nine more,
and there is never an end.
All the other overwhelming colors,
in company with the years, kept leaving me,
and now alone remains
the amorphous light, the inextricable shadow
and the gold of the beginning.
O sunsets, O tigers, O wonders
of myth and epic,
O gold more dear to me, gold of your hair
which these hands long to touch.

East Lansing, 1972

—A.R.

EL SUEÑO

Cuando los relojes de la media noche prodiguen
Un tiempo generoso,
Iré más lejos que los bogavantes de Ulises
A la región del sueño, inaccesible
A la memoria humana.
De esa región inmersa rescato restos
Que no acabo de comprender:
Hierbas de sencilla botánica,
Animales algo diversos,
Diálogos con los muertos,
Rostros que realmente son máscaras,
Palabras de lenguajes muy antiguos
Y a veces un horror incomparable
Al que nos puede dar el día.
Seré todos o nadie. Seré el otro
Que sin saberlo soy, el que ha mirado
Ese otro sueño, mi vigilia. La juzga,
Resignado y sonriente.

THE DREAM

While the clocks of the midnight hours are squandering
an abundance of time,
I shall go, farther than the shipmates of Ulysses,
to the territory of dream, beyond the reach
of human memory.
From that underwater world I save some fragments,
inexhaustible to my understanding:
grasses from some primitive botany,
animals of all kinds,
conversations with the dead,
faces which all the time are masks,
words out of very ancient languages,
and at times, horror, unlike anything
the day can offer us.
I shall be all or no one. I shall be the other
I am without knowing it, he who has looked on
that other dream, my waking state. He weighs it up,
resigned and smiling.

—A.R.

EL SUICIDA

No quedará en la noche una estrella.
No quedará la noche.
Moriré y conmigo la suma
Del intolerable universo.
Borraré las pirámides, las medallas,
Los continentes y las caras.
Borraré la acumulación del pasado.
Haré polvo la historia, polvo el polvo.
Estoy mirando el último poniente.
Oigo el último pájaro.
Lego la nada a nadie.

THE SUICIDE

Not a single star will be left in the night.
The night will not be left.
I will die and, with me,
the weight of the intolerable universe.
I shall erase the pyramids, the medallions,
the continents and faces.
I shall erase the accumulated past.
I shall make dust of history, dust of dust.
Now I am looking on the final sunset.
I am hearing the last bird.
I bequeath nothingness to no one.

—A.R.

ELEGÍA

Tres muy antiguas caras me desvelan:
Una el Océano, que habló con Claudio,
Otra el Norte de aceros ignorantes
Y atroces en la aurora y el ocaso,
La tercera la muerte, ese otro nombre
Del incesante tiempo que nos roe.
La carga secular de los ayeres
De la historia que fue o que fue soñada
Me abruma, personal como una culpa.
Pienso en la nave ufana que devuelve
A los mares el cuerpo de Scyld Sceaving
Que reinó en Dinamarca bajo el cielo;
Pienso en el alto lobo, cuyas riendas
Eran sierpes, que dio al barco incendiado
la blancura del dios hermoso y muerto;
Pienso en piratas cuya carne humana
Es dispersión y limo bajo el peso
De los mares que fueron su aventura;
Pienso en las tumbas que los navegantes
Vieron desde boreales Odiseas.
Pienso en mi propia, en mi perfecta muerte,
Sin la urna cineraria y sin la lágrima.

ELEGY

Three very ancient faces stay with me:
one is the Ocean, which would talk with Claudius,
another the North, with its unfeeling temper,
savage both at sunrise and at sunset;
the third is Death, that other name we give
to passing time, which wears us all away.
The secular burden of those yesterdays
from history which happened or was dreamed,
oppresses me as personally as guilt.
I think of the proud ship, carrying back
to sea the body of Scyld Sceaving,
who ruled in Denmark underneath the sky;
I think of the great wolf, whose reins were serpents,
who lent the burning boat the purity
and whiteness of the beautiful dead god;
I think of pirates too, whose human flesh
is scattered through the slime beneath the weight
of waters which were ground for their adventures;
I think of mausoleums which the sailors
saw in the course of Northern odysseys.
I think of my own death, my perfect death,
without a funeral urn, without a tear.

—A.R.

THE UNENDING ROSE

A Susana Bombal

A los quinientos años de la Héjira
Persia miró desde sus alminares
La invasión de las lanzas del desierto
Y Attar de Nishapur miró una rosa
Y le dijo con tácita palabra
Como el que piensa, no como el que reza:
—Tu vaga esfera está en mi mano. El tiempo
Nos encorva a los dos y nos ignora
En esta tarde de un jardín perdido.
Tu leve peso es húmedo en el aire.
La incesante pleamar de tu fragancia
Sube a mi vieja cara que declina
Pero te sé más lejos que aquel niño
Que te entrevió en las láminas de un sueño
O aquí en este jardín, una mañana.
La blancura del sol puede ser tuya
O el oro de la luna o la bermeja
Firmeza de la espada en la victoria.
Soy ciego y nada sé, pero preveo
Que son más los caminos. Cada cosa
Es infinitas cosas. Eres música,
Firmamentos, palacios, ríos, ángeles,
Rosa profunda, ilimitada, íntima,
Que el Señor mostrará a mis ojos muertos.

THE UNENDING ROSE

To Susana Bombal

Five hundred years in the wake of the Hegira,
Persia looked down from its minarets
on the invasion of the desert lances,
and Attar of Nishapur gazed on a rose,
addressing it in words that had no sound,
as one who thinks rather than one who prays:
"Your fragile globe is in my hand; and time
is bending both of us, both unaware,
this afternoon, in a forgotten garden.
Your brittle shape is humid in the air.
The steady, tidal fullness of your fragrance
rises up to my old, declining face.
But I know you far longer than that child
who glimpsed you in the layers of a dream
or here, in this garden, once upon a morning.
The whiteness of the sun may well be yours
or the moon's gold, or else the crimson stain
on the hard sword-edge in the victory.
I am blind and I know nothing, but I see
there are more ways to go; and everything
is an infinity of things. You, you are music,
rivers, firmaments, palaces, and angels,
O endless rose, intimate, without limit,
which the Lord will finally show to my dead eyes."

—A.R.

EIN TRAUM

Lo sabían los tres.
Ella era la compañera de Kafka.
Kafka la había soñado.
Lo sabían los tres.
Él era el amigo de Kafka.
Kafka lo había soñado.
Lo sabían los tres.
La mujer le dijo al amigo:
Quiero que esta noche me quieras.
Lo sabían los tres.
El hombre le contestó: Si pecamos,
Kafka dejará de soñarnos.
Uno lo supo.
No había nadie más en la tierra.
Kafka se dijo:
Ahora que se fueron los dos, he quedado solo.
Dejaré de soñarme.

EIN TRAUM

All three of them knew.
She was Kafka's sweetheart.
Kafka had dreamed her.
All three of them knew.
He was Kafka's friend.
Kafka had dreamed him.
All three of them knew.
The woman said to the friend:
I want you to love me tonight.
All three of them knew.
The man replied: If we sin,
Kafka will stop dreaming us.
One of them knew.
There was no one else on earth.
Kafka said to himself:
Now that those two are gone, I'm left alone.
I shall stop dreaming myself.

—s.k.

SIGNOS

A Susana Bombal

*Hacia 1915, en Ginebra, vi en la terraza de un
museo una alta campana con caracteres chinos.
En 1976 escribo estas líneas:*

Indescifrada y sola, sé que puedo
ser en la vaga noche una plegaria
de bronce o la sentencia en que se cifra
el sabor de una vida o de una tarde
o el sueño de Chuang Tzu, que ya conoces
o una fecha trivial o una parábola
o un vasto emperador, hoy unas sílabas,
o el universo o tu secreto nombre
o aquel enigma que indagaste en vano
a lo largo del tiempo y de sus días.
Puedo ser todo. Déjame en la sombra.

SIGNS

for Susana Bombal

Around 1915, in Geneva, I saw on the terrace
of a museum a tall bell with Chinese characters.
In 1976 I write these lines:

Undeciphered and alone, I know
in the vague night I can be a bronze
prayer or a saying in which is encoded
the flavor of a life or of an evening
or Chuang Tzu's dream, which you know already,
or an insignificant date or a parable
or a great emperor, now a few syllables,
or the universe or your secret name
or that enigma you investigated in vain
for so long a time through all your days.
I can be anything. Leave me in the dark.

—S.K.

ENDIMIÓN EN LATMOS

Yo dormía en la cumbre y era hermoso
mi cuerpo, que los años han gastado.
Alto en la noche helénica, el centauro
demoraba su cuádruple carrera
para atisbar mi sueño. Me placía
dormir para soñar y para el otro
sueño lustral que elude la memoria
y que nos purifica del gravamen
de ser aquel que somos en la tierra.
Diana, la diosa, que es también la luna,
me veía dormir en la montaña
y lentamente descendió a mis brazos
oro y amor en la encendida noche.
Yo apretaba los párpados mortales,
yo quería no ver el rostro bello
que mis labios de polvo profanaban.
Yo aspiré la fragancia de la luna
y su infinita voz dijo mi nombre.
Oh las puras mejillas que se buscan,
oh ríos del amor y de la noche,
oh el beso humano y la tensión del arco.
No sé cuánto duraron mis venturas;
hay cosas que no miden los racimos
ni la flor ni la nieve delicada.
La gente me rehúye. Le da miedo
el hombre que fue amado por la luna.
Los años han pasado. Una zozobra
da horror a mi vigilia. Me pregunto
si aquel tumulto de oro en la montaña
fue verdadero o no fue más que un sueño.
Inútil repetirme que el recuerdo

ENDYMION ON LATMOS

I was sleeping on the mountain top
and spent by the years my body was lovely.
Deep in the Hellenic night, the centaur
paused in his quadruple race
to spy on my sleep. It was a pleasure
to sleep in order to dream, and to seek the other
lustral sleep that eludes memory
and cleanses us of the burden
of being who we are on earth.
Diana, the goddess who is also the moon,
saw me sleeping on the mountain
and slowly descended into my arms.
Gold and love in a night ablaze.
I pressed fingers to my mortal eyelids
I wanted not to see the lovely face
my lips of clay were profaning.
I breathed in the fragrance of the moon
and her infinite voice spoke my name.
Oh, the pure, sought after cheeks.
Oh rivers of love and of night.
Oh the human kiss and tensed bow.
I don't know how long the bliss lasted.
There are things not measured by grape
or flower or delicate snow
People flee from me, afraid
of the man who was loved by the moon.
The years have passed. An inner anguish
brings horror to my sleeplessness. I ask myself
if that tumult of gold on the mountain
was true, or only a dream.
Useless to tell myself that a dream

de ayer y un sueño son la misma cosa.
Mi soledad recorre los comunes
caminos de la tierra, pero siempre
busco en la antigua noche de los númenes
la indiferente luna, hija de Zeus.

JORGE LUIS BORGES

and the memory of yesterday are the same thing.
My solitude wanders the ordinary
roads of earth, but I always search
the ancient night of the spirits
for the daughter of Zeus, the indifferent moon.

—C.M.

NI SIQUIERA SOY POLVO

No quiero ser quien soy. La avara suerte
Me ha deparado el siglo diecisiete,
El polvo y la rutina de Castilla,
Las cosas repetidas, la mañana
Que, prometiendo el hoy, nos da la víspera,
La plática del cura y del barbero,
La soledad que va dejando el tiempo
Y una vaga sobrina analfabeta.
Soy hombre entrado en años. Una página
Casual me reveló no usadas voces
Que me buscaban, Amadís y Urganda.
Vendí mis tierras y compré los libros
Que historian cabalmente las empresas:
El Grial, que recogió la sangre humana
Que el Hijo derramó para salvarnos,
El ídolo de oro de Mahoma,
Los hierros, las almenas, las banderas
Y las operaciones de la magia.
Cristianos caballeros recorrían
Los reinos de la tierra, vindicando
El honor ultrajado o imponiendo
Justicia con los filos de la espada.
Quiera Dios que un enviado restituya
A nuestro tiempo ese ejercico noble.
Mis sueños lo divisan. Lo he sentido
A veces en mi triste carne célibe.
No sé aún su nombre. Yo, Quijano,
Seré ese paladín. Seré mi sueño.
En esta vieja casa hay una adarga
Antigua y una hoja de Toledo
Y una lanza y los libros verdaderos
Que a mi brazo prometen la victoria.
¿A mi brazo? Mi cara (que no he visto)

I AM NOT EVEN DUST

I do not want to be who I am. Petty luck
Has offered me the seventeenth century,
The dust and constitution of Castile,
The things that come and come again, the morning
That, promising today, gives us the evening,
The patter of the barber and the priest,
The loneliness that time continues leaving
And one illiterate and idle niece.
I am a man of years. A casual page
Revealed the unused voices that had been
Pursuing me, Urganda and Amadís.
I sold my acres and procured the books
That recollect completely the campaigns:
The Grail, which received the human blood
Poured out for our salvation by the Son,
The idol of Mohammed, made of gold,
The parapets, the battlements, the banners
And all the operations of the magic.
The knights of Christianity spilled over
The kingdoms of the world, to vindicate
Insulted dignity, or to impose
Justice with the edges of a sword.
Please God, let one be sent to reinstate
That noble practice in our century.
My dreams anticipate it. I have felt it
At moments in my celibate, sad flesh.
I don't yet know his name. But I, Quijano,
Will be that champion. I will be my dream.
In this historic house there is a shield
Of long ago and a stainless blade of Toledo
And an authentic lance and the true books
That promise to my arm full victory.
To my arm? My visage (which I have not seen)

No proyecta una cara en el espejo.
Ni siquiera soy polvo. Soy un sueño
Que entreteje en el sueño y la vigilia
Mi hermano y padre, el capitán Cervantes,
Que militó en los mares de Lepanto
Y supo unos latines y algo de árabe . . .
Para que yo pueda soñar al otro
Cuya verde memoria será parte
De los días del hombre, te suplico:
Mi Dios, mi soñador, sigue soñándome.

Has never cast its image in the mirror.
I am not even dust. I am a dream
That weaves itself in sleep and wakefulness.
My brother and my father, Captain Cervantes,
Fought nobly on the waters of Lepanto,
Learned Latin and a little Arabic . . .
That I might be allowed to dream the other
Whose fertile memory will be a part
Of all the days of man, I humbly pray:
My God, my dreamer, keep on dreaming me.

— E.M.

UN SÁBADO

Un hombre ciego en una casa hueca
Fatiga ciertos limitados rumbos
Y toca las paredes que se alargan
Y el cristal de las puertas interiores
Y los ásperos lomos de los libros
Vedados a su amor y la apagada
Platería que fue de los mayores
Y los grifos del agua y las molduras
Y unas vagas monedas y la llave.
Está solo y no hay nadie en el espejo.
Ir y venir. La mano roza el borde
Del primer anaquel. Sin proponérselo,
Se ha tendido en la cama solitaria
Y siente que los actos que ejecuta
Interminablemente en su crepúsculo
Obedecen a un juego que no entiende
Y que dirige un dios indescifrable.
En voz alta repite y cadenciosa
Fragmentos de los clásicos y ensaya
Variaciones de verbos y de epítetos
Y bien o mal escribe este poema.

A SATURDAY

A blind man living in a hollow house
Exhausts his certain narrow corridors
And puts his hands on the expansive walls
And the smooth glass of the interior doors
And the rough-textured bindings of the books
Forbidden to his love and the unpolished
Silver that belonged to his ancestors
And the old water spigots and the moldings
And one or two stray pennies and the key.
He is alone and no one is in the mirror.
Going or coming. His knuckles graze the border
Of the first shelf. Without deciding to
He has stretched out on the solitary bed
And senses that the acts he executes
Interminably in his twilit hour
Obey a game he doesn't understand
And that an enigmatic god conducts.
In a loud voice he rhythmically repeats
Some fragments from the classics and rehearses
Variations of verbs and epithets
And, good or bad, at last he writes this poem.

—E.M.

ADÁN ES TU CENIZA

La espada morirá como el racimo.
El cristal no es más frágil que la roca.
Las cosas son su porvenir de polvo.
El hierro es el orín. La voz, el eco.
Adán, el joven padre, es tu ceniza.
El último jardín será el primero.
El ruiseñor y Píndaro son voces.
La aurora es el reflejo del ocaso.
El micenio, la máscara de oro.
El alto muro, la ultrajada ruina.
Urquiza, lo que dejan los puñales.
El rostro que se mira en el espejo
No es el de ayer. La noche lo ha gastado.
El delicado tiempo nos modela.

Qué dicha ser el agua invulnerable
Que corre en la parábola de Heráclito
O el intrincado fuego, pero ahora,
En este largo día que no pasa,
Me siento duradero y desvalido.

ADAM IS YOUR ASHES

The sword will die just like the ripening cluster.
The glass is no more fragile than the rock.
All things are their own prophecy of dust.
Iron is rust. The voice, already echo.
Adam, the youthful father, is your ashes.
The final garden will also be the first.
The nightingale and Pindar both are voices.
The dawn is a reflection of the sunset.
The Mycenaean, his burial mask of gold.
The highest wall, the humiliated ruin.
Urquiza, he whom daggers left behind.
The face that looks upon itself in the mirror
Is not the face of yesterday. The night
Has spent it. Delicate time has molded us.

What joy to be the invulnerable water
That ran assuredly through the parable
Of Heraclitus, or the intricate fire,
But now, on this long day that doesn't end,
I feel irrevocable and alone.

—E.M.

III.

WAITING FOR
THE NIGHT
(1978–1985)

HISTORIA DE LA NOCHE

A lo largo de sus generaciones
los hombres erigieron la noche.
En el principio era ceguera y sueño
y espinas que laceran el pie desnudo
y temor de los lobos.
Nunca sabremos quién forjó la palabra
para el intervalo de sombra
que divide los dos crepúsculos;
nunca sabremos en qué siglo fue cifra
del espacio de estrellas.
Otros engendraron el mito.
La hicieron madre de las Parcas tranquilas
que tejen el destino
y le sacrificaban ovejas negras
y el gallo que presagia su fin.
Doce casas le dieron los caldeos;
infinitos mundos, el Pórtico.
Hexámetros latinos la modelaron
y el terror de Pascal.
Luis de León vio en ella la patria
de su alma estremecida.
Ahora la sentimos inagotable
como un antiguo vino
y nadie puede contemplarla sin vértigo
y el tiempo la ha cargado de eternidad.

Y pensar que no existiría
sin esos tenues instrumentos, los ojos.

HISTORY OF THE NIGHT

Down through the generations
men built the night.
In the beginning it was blindness and sleep
and thorns that tear the naked foot
and fear of wolves.
We shall never know who forged the word
for the interval of shadow
which divides the two twilights;
we shall never know in what century it stood as a cipher
for the space between the stars.
Other men engendered the myth.
They made it mother of the tranquil Fates
who weave destiny,
and sacrificed black sheep to it
and the cock which presages its end.
The Chaldeans gave it twelve houses;
infinite worlds, the Gateway.
Latin hexameters gave it form
and the terror of Pascal.
Luis de León saw in it the fatherland
of his shuddering soul.
Now we feel it to be inexhaustible
like an ancient wine
and no one can contemplate it without vertigo
and time has charged it with eternity.

And to think it would not exist
but for those tenuous instruments, the eyes.

         —C.T.

LA JOVEN NOCHE

Ya las lustrales aguas de la noche me absuelven
de los muchos colores y de las muchas formas.
Ya en el jardín las aves y los astros exaltan
el regreso anhelado de las antiguas normas
del sueño y de la sombra. Ya la sombra ha sellado
los espejos que copian la ficción de las cosas.
Mejor lo dijo Goethe: *Lo cercano se aleja.*
Esas cuatro palabras cifran todo el crepúsculo.
En el jardín las rosas dejan de ser las rosas
y quieren ser la Rosa.

THE YOUNG NIGHT

And now the lustral waters of night absolve me
from the many colors and the many forms.
In the garden, birds and stars exalt
the longed-for return of the ancient norms
of sleep and shadow. Darkness is sealing
the mirrors which copy the fiction of things.
Goethe said it best: *everything near becomes far*.
Those four words capture the entire twilight.
In the garden, roses cease to be roses;
they wish to be the Rose.

—C.M.

DOS FORMAS DEL INSOMNIO

¿Qué es el insomnio?

La pregunta es retórica; sé demasiado bien la respuesta.

Es temer y contar en la alta noche las duras campanadas fatales, es ensayar con magia inútil una respiración regular, es la carga de un cuerpo que bruscamente cambia de lado, es apretar los párpados, es un estado parecido a la fiebre y que ciertamente no es la vigilia, es pronunciar fragmentos de párrafos leídos hace ya muchos años, es saberse culpable de velar cuando los otros duermen, es querer hundirse en el sueño y no poder hundirse en el sueño, es el horror de ser y de seguir siendo, es el alba dudosa.

¿Qué es la longevidad?

Es el horror de ser en un cuerpo humano cuyas facultades declinan, es un insomnio que se mide por décadas y no con agujas de acero, es el peso de mares y de pirámides, de antiguas bibliotecas y dinastías, de las auroras que vio Adán, es no ignorar que estoy condenado a mi carne, a mi detestada voz, a mi nombre, a una rutina de recuerdos, al castellano, que no sé manejar, a la nostalgia del latín, que no sé, a querer hundirme en la muerte y no poder hundirme en la muerte, a ser y seguir siendo.

TWO FORMS OF INSOMNIA

What is insomnia?

The question is rhetorical. I know the answer only too well. It is to count off and dread in the small hours the fateful harsh strokes of the chime. It is attempting with ineffectual magic to breathe smoothly. It is the burden of a body that abruptly shifts sides. It is shutting the eyelids down tight. It is a state like fever and is assuredly not watchfulness. It is saying over bits of paragraphs read years and years before. It is knowing how guilty you are to be lying awake when others are asleep. It is trying to sink into slumber and being unable to sink into slumber. It is the horror of being and going on being. It is the dubious daybreak.

What is longevity? It is the horror of existing in a human body whose faculties are in decline. It is insomnia measured by decades and not by metal hands. It is carrying the weight of seas and pyramids, of ancient libraries and dynasties, of the dawns that Adam saw. It is being well aware that I am bound to my flesh, to a voice I detest, to my name, to routinely remembering, to Castilian, over which I have no control, to feeling nostalgic for the Latin I do not know. It is trying to sink into death and being unable to sink into death. It is being and continuing to be.

—A.S.T.

POEMA

Dormías. Te despierto.
La gran mañana depara la ilusión de un principio.
Te habías olvidado de Virgilio. Ahí están los hexámetros.
Te traigo muchas cosas.
Las cuatro raíces del griego: la tierra, el agua, el fuego, el aire.
Un solo nombre de mujer.
La amistad de la luna.
Los claros colores del atlas.
El olvido, que purifica.
La memoria que elige y que redescubre.
El hábito que nos ayuda a sentir que somos inmortales.
La esfera y las agujas que parcelan el inasible tiempo.
La fragancia del sándalo.
Las dudas que llamamos, no sin alguna vanidad, metafísica.
La curva del bastón que tu mano espera.
El sabor de las uvas y de la miel.

POEM

You were asleep. I wake you.
The vast morning brings the illusion of a beginning.
You had forgotten Virgil. Here are the hexameters.
I bring you many things.
The four Greek elements: earth, water, fire, air.
The single name of a woman.
The friendship of the moon.
The bright colors of the atlas.
Forgetting, which purifies.
Memory, which chooses and rediscovers.
The habits which help us feel we are immortal.
The sphere and the hands that measure elusive time.
The fragrance of sandalwood.
The doubts that we call, not without some vanity,
    metaphysics.
The curve of the walking stick the hand anticipates.
The taste of grapes and of honey.

REVERSO

Recordar a quien duerme
es un acto común y cotidiano
que podría hacernos temblar.
Recordar a quien duerme
es imponer a otro la interminable
prisión del universo
de su tiempo sin ocaso ni aurora.
Es revelarle que es alguien o algo
que está sujeto a un nombre que lo publica
y a un cúmulo de ayeres.
Es inquietar su eternidad.
Es cargarlo de siglos y de estrellas.
Es restituir al tiempo otro Lázaro
cargado de memoria.
Es infamar el agua del Leteo.

REVERSE

To wake someone from sleep
is a common day-to-day act
that can set us trembling.
To wake someone from sleep
is to saddle some other with the interminable
prison of the universe
of his time, with neither sunset nor dawn.
It is to show him he is someone or something
subject to a name that lays claim to him
and an accumulation of yesterdays.
It is to trouble his eternity,
to load him down with centuries and stars,
to restore to time another Lazarus
burdened with memory.
It is to desecrate the waters of Lethe.

—A.R.

YESTERDAYS

De estirpe de pastores protestantes
y de soldados sudamericanos
que opusieron al godo y a las lanzas
del desierto su polvo incalculable,
soy y no soy. Mi verdadera estirpe
es la voz, que aún escucho, de mi padre,
conmemorando música de Swinburne,
y los grandes volúmenes que he hojeado,
hojeado y no leído, y que me bastan.
Soy lo que me contaron los filósofos.
El azar o el destino, esos dos nombres
de una secreta cosa que ignoramos,
me prodigaron patrias: Buenos Aires,
Nara, donde pasé una sola noche,
Ginebra, las dos Córdobas, Islandia . . .
Soy el cóncavo sueño solitario
en que me pierdo o trato de perderme,
la servidumbre de los dos crepúsculos,
las antiguas mañanas, la primera
vez que vi el mar o una ignorante luna,
sin su Virgilio y sin su Galileo.
Soy cada instante de mi largo tiempo,
cada noche de insomnio escrupuloso,
cada separación y cada víspera.
Soy la errónea memoria de un grabado
que hay en la habitación y que mis ojos,
hoy apagados, vieron claramente:
El Jinete, la Muerte y el Demonio.
Soy aquel otro que miró el desierto
y que en su eternidad sigue mirándolo.
Soy un espejo, un eco. El epitafio.

YESTERDAYS

From a lineage of Protestant ministers
and South American soldiers
who fought, with their incalculable dust,
against the Spaniards and the desert's lances,
I am and I am not. My true lineage
is the voice, which I can still hear, of my father
celebrating Swinburne's music,
and the great volumes I have leafed through,
leafed through and never read, which was enough.
I am whatever the philosophers told me.
Chance or destiny, those two names
for a secret thing we'll never understand,
lavished me with homelands: Buenos Aires,
Nara, where I spent a single night,
Geneva, Iceland, the two Córdobas . . .
I am the hollow solitary dream
in which I lose or try to lose myself,
the bondage between two twilights,
the old mornings, the first
time I saw the sea or an ignorant moon,
without its Virgil or its Galileo.
I am every instant of my lengthy time,
every night of scrupulous insomnia,
every parting and every night before.
I am the faulty memory of an engraving
that's still here in the room and that my eyes,
now darkened, once saw clearly:
The Knight, Death, and the Devil.
I am that other one who saw the desert
and in its eternity goes on watching it.
I am a mirror, an echo. The epitaph.

—S.K.

EL SUEÑO

La noche nos impone su tarea
mágica. Destejer el universo,
las ramificaciones infinitas
de efectos y de causas, que se pierden
en ese vértigo sin fondo, el tiempo.
La noche quiere que esta noche olvides
tu nombre, tus mayores y tu sangre,
cada palabra humana y cada lágrima,
lo que pudo enseñarte la vigilia,
el ilusorio punto de los geómetras,
la línea, el plano, el cubo, la pirámide,
el cilindro, la esfera, el mar, las olas,
tu mejilla en la almohada, la frescura
de la sábana nueva, los jardines,
los imperios, los Césares y Shakespeare
y lo que es más difícil, lo que amas.
Curiosamente, una pastilla puede
borrar el cosmos y erigir el caos.

SLEEP

The night assigns us its magic
task. To unravel the universe,
the infinite ramifications
of effects and causes, all lost
in that bottomless vertigo, time.
Tonight the night wants you to forget
your name, your elders and your blood,
every human word and every tear,
what you would have learned from staying awake,
the illusory point of the geometricians,
the line, the plane, the cube, the pyramid,
the cylinder, the sphere, the sea, the waves,
your cheek on the pillow, the coolness
of the fresh sheet, gardens,
empires, the Caesars and Shakespeare
and the hardest thing of all, what you love.
Oddly enough, a pill can
erase the cosmos and erect chaos.

—S.K.

LOS SUEÑOS

Mi cuerpo físico puede estar en Lucerna, en Colorado o en El Cairo, pero al despertarme cada mañana, al retomar el hábito de ser Borges, emerjo invariablemente de un sueño que ocurre en Buenos Aires. Las imágenes pueden ser cordilleras, ciénagas con andamios, escaleras de caracol que se hunden en sótanos, médanos cuya arena debo contar, pero cualquiera de esas cosas es una bocacalle precisa del barrio de Palermo o del Sur. En la vigilia estoy siempre en el centro de una vaga neblina luminosa de tinte gris o azul; veo en los sueños o converso con muertos, sin que ninguna de esas dos cosas me asombre. Nunca sueño con el presente sino con un Buenos Aires pretérito y con las galerías y claraboyas de la Biblioteca Nacional en la calle México. ¿Quiere todo esto decir que, más allá de mi voluntad y de mi conciencia, soy irreparablemente, incomprensiblemente porteño?

UN SUEÑO

En un desierto lugar del Irán hay una no muy alta torre de piedra, sin puerta ni ventana. En la única habitación (cuyo piso es de tierra y que tiene la forma del círculo) hay una mesa de madera y un banco. En esa celda circular, un hombre que se parece a mí escribe en caracteres que no comprendo un largo poema sobre un hombre que en otra celda circular escribe un poema sobre un hombre que en otra celda circular . . . El proceso no tiene fin y nadie podrá leer lo que los prisioneros escriben.

JORGE LUIS BORGES

DREAMS

My physical body may be in Lucerne, in Colorado or in Cairo, but each morning when I awake, when I once again take on the habit of being Borges, I invariably emerge from a dream which takes place in Buenos Aires. Whether the dream-images involve sierras, or swamps with stilt huts, spiral staircases sunk in cellars, sand dunes whose grains of sand I must perforce count, all of them are a particular cross street in Buenos Aires: in the Palermo or Sur quarter. When I am sleepless I am always at the center of a vague luminous haze, gray or blue in hue. Asleep, in my dreams, I see or converse with the dead. None of these things surprises me in the least. I never dream in the present but only of a past-tense Buenos Aires, and of the galleries and skylights of the National Library on Mexico Street. Does all this mean that beyond the limits of my will and consciousness I am, irreparably, incomprehensibly, a *porteño,* a native-born descendant of the people of the port of Buenos Aires?

—A.K.

A DREAM

In a deserted place in Iran there is a not very tall stone tower that has neither door nor window. In the only room (with a dirt floor and shaped like a circle) there is a wooden table and a bench. In that circular cell, a man who looks like me is writing in letters I cannot understand a long poem about a man who in another circular cell is writing a poem about a man who in another circular cell . . . The process never ends and no one will be able to read what the prisoners write.

—S.J.L.

ALGUIEN SOÑARÁ

¿Qué soñará el indescifrable futuro? Soñará que Alonso Quijano puede ser don Quijote sin dejar su aldea y sus libros. Soñará que una víspera de Ulises puede ser más pródiga que el poema que narra sus trabajos. Soñará generaciones humanas que no reconocerán el nombre de Ulises. Soñará sueños más precisos que la vigilia de hoy. Soñará que podremos hacer milagros y que no los haremos, porque será más real imaginarlos. Soñará mundos tan intensos que la voz de una sola de sus aves podría matarte. Soñará que el olvido y la memoria pueden ser actos voluntarios, no agresiones o dádivas del azar. Soñará que veremos con todo el cuerpo, como quería Milton desde la sombra de esos tiernos orbes, los ojos. Soñará un mundo sin la máquina y sin esa doliente máquina, el cuerpo. La vida no es un sueño pero puede llegar a ser un sueño, escribe Novalis.

SOMEONE WILL DREAM

What will the indecipherable future dream? A dream that Alonso Quijano can be Don Quixote without leaving his village and his books. A dream that the eve of Ulysses can be more prodigious than the poem that recounts his hardships. Dreaming human generations that will not recognize the name of Ulysses. Dreaming dreams more precise than today's wakefulness. A dream that we will be able to do miracles and that we won't do them, because it will be more real to imagine them. Dreaming worlds so intense that the voice of one bird could kill you. Dreaming that to forget and to remember can be voluntary actions, not aggressions or gifts of chance. A dream that we shall see with our whole body, as Milton wished from the shadow of those tender orbs, his eyes. Dreaming a world without machines and without that afflicted machine, the body. Life is not a dream, Novalis writes, but can become a dream.

—S.J.L.

SUEÑO SOÑADO EN EDIMBURGO

Antes del alba soñé un sueño que me dejó abrumado y que trataré de ordenar.

Tus mayores te engendran. En la otra frontera de los desiertos hay unas aulas polvorientas o, si se quiere, unos depósitos polvorientos, y en esas aulas o depósitos hay filas paralelas de pizarrones cuya longitud se mide por leguas o por leguas de leguas y en los que alguien ha trazado con tiza letras y números. Se ignora cuántos pizarrones hay en conjunto pero se entiende que son muchos y que algunos están abarrotados y otros casi vacíos. Las puertas de los muros son corredizas, a la manera del Japón, y están hechas de un metal oxidado. El edificio entero es circular, pero es tan enorme que desde afuera no se advierte la menor curvatura y lo que se ve es una recta. Los apretados pizarrones son más altos que un hombre y alcanzan hasta el cielo raso de yeso, que es blanquecino o gris. En el costado izquierdo del pizarrón hay primero palabras y después números. Las palabras se ordenan verticalmente, como en un diccionario. La primera es *Aar,* el río de Berna. La siguen los guarismos arábigos, cuya cifra es indefinida pero seguramente no infinita. Indican el número preciso de veces que verás aquel río, el número preciso de veces que lo descubrirás en el mapa, el número preciso de veces que soñarás con él. La última palabra es acaso *Zwingli* y queda muy lejos. En otro desmedido pizarrón esta inscrita *neverness* y al lado de esa extraña palabra hay ahora una cifra. Todo el decurso de tu vida está en esos signos.

No hay un segundo que no esté royendo una serie.

A DREAM IN EDINBURGH

Just before dawn I had a dream that left me quite befogged. I will try to make it intelligible.

Your ancestors bring you into being. On the far frontiers of the living desert there are some dusty public spaces, rather like vast sandy warehouses; and in these spaces, or stores, there are parallel rows of blackboards, stretching for leagues, for leagues of leagues, some of them with chalked lettering and numbers. Impossible to guess how many—certainly an enormous number—some of them covered with writing, others almost empty. Set in the walls were sliding doors, in the Japanese manner, made of some rusted metal. Each place was vast and circular, so enormous that from the outside its walls showed no trace of curvature. It all seemed one straight line. The voluminous blackboards are taller than a man and seem to reach up to a plaster-colored, greyish-white sky. On the left side of the blackboards, words are listed first, then numbers. The words are arranged alphabetically, as in a dictionary. The first word is *Arr*, a river in Bern. It is followed by words in Arabic script that, while indecipherable, are certainly not arbitrary. They spell out the following: the precise number of times you have laid eyes on that river, the specific occasions on which you have come across it on a map, the exact instances of your dreaming about it. The last word in the index is, by chance, *Zwingli*; and in that list it is very far away. One demented entry is inscribed *neverness*; and next to that strange word is written a cipher. The whole unwinding of your lived life is somewhere recorded in these scribbles.

There is not a single second that is not gnawing away at all our previous orderings.

Agotarás la cifra que corresponde al sabor del jengibre y seguirás viviendo. Agotarás la cifra que corresponde a la lisura del cristal y seguirás viviendo unos días. Agotarás la cifra de los latidos que te han sido fijados y entonces habrás muerto.

EL CABALLO

La llanura que espera desde el principio. Más allá de los últimos duraznos, junto a las aguas, un gran caballo blanco de ojos dormidos parece llenar la mañana. El cuello arqueado, como en una lámina persa, y la crin y la cola arremolinadas. Es recto y firme y está hecho de largas curvas. Recuerdo la curiosa línea de Chaucer: *a very horsely horse*. No hay con qué compararlo y no está cerca, pero se sabe que es muy alto.

Nada, salvo ya el mediodía.

Aquí y ahora está el caballo, pero algo distinto hay en él, porque también es un caballo en un sueño de Alejandro de Macedonia.

You will eventually discover the sign that stands for the savor of ginger, and that will keep you going. You'll work out the icon that corresponds exactly to the clarity of crystal. That too will win you some continuing life. But when you eventually check the number of heartbeats already allotted to you for your lifetime, you will already be dead.

—A.R.

THE HORSE

The plain that awaits from the beginning. Beyond the last of the peach trees, by the waters, a great white horse with sleepy eyes appears to fill the morning. Neck arched, as in a Persian miniature, and the mane, and the tail, swirling. It is firm and upright, made of long curves. I remember the curious line by Chaucer: *a very horsely horse*. There is nothing to compare it to, and though it is not nearby, one can tell it is tall.

Nothing, yet it is now midday.

The horse is here and now, but there is something different about it, it is also a horse in a dream by Alexander of Macedonia.

—J.K.

UNA PESADILLA

Cerré la puerta de mi departamento y me dirigí al ascensor. Iba a llamarlo cuando un personaje rarísimo ocupó toda mi atención. Era tan alto que yo debí haber comprendido que lo soñaba. Aumentaba su estatura un bonete cónico. Su rostro (que no vi nunca de perfil) tenía algo de tártaro o de lo que yo imagino que es tártaro y terminaba en una barba negra, que también era cónica. Los ojos me miraban burlonamente. Usaba un largo sobretodo negro y lustroso, lleno de grandes discos blancos. Casi tocaba el suelo. Acaso sospechando que soñaba, me atreví a preguntarle no sé en qué idioma por qué vestía de esa manera. Me sonrió con sorna y se desabrochó el sobretodo. Vi que debajo había un largo traje enterizo del mismo material y con los mismos discos blancos, y supe (como se saben las cosas en los sueños) que debajo había otro.

En aquel preciso momento sentí el inconfundible sabor de la pesadilla y me desperté.

A NIGHTMARE

I closed the door to my apartment and walked to the elevator. I was about to press the call button when a truly startling person arrested my attention. He was so tall that I should have understood that I was dreaming him. His stature was increased by a cone-shaped cap. His face (which I never saw in profile) had about it something of the Tatar, or what I imagine a Tatar to be, and it ended in a black beard, also cone shaped. His eyes gazed at me in a mocking manner. He was dressed in a long overcoat, black and glossy, covered with large white discs. It reached nearly to the floor. With a suspicion that perhaps I was dreaming, I ventured to ask him, in some language or other, why he was dressed in such a fashion. He gave me an ironic smile and unbuttoned his overcoat. I saw that under it was a long one-piece suit in the same material and covered with the same white discs, and I realized (in the way one does in dreams) that under it there would be another one.

At that exact moment I tasted the unmistakable savor of nightmare, and awoke.

—A.K.

DOOMSDAY

Será cuando la trompeta resuene, como escribe San Juan el
    Teólogo.
Ha sido en 1757, según el testimonio de Swedenborg.
Fue en Israel (cuando la loba clavó en la cruz la carne de
    Cristo), pero no sólo entonces.
Ocurre en cada pulsación de tu sangre.
No hay un instante que no pueda ser el cráter del Infierno.
No hay un instante que no pueda ser el agua del Paraíso.
No hay un instante que no esté cargado como un arma.
En cada instante puedes ser Caín o Siddharta, la máscara o el
    rostro.
En cada instante puede revelarte su amor Helena de Troya.
En cada instante el gallo puede haber cantado tres veces.
En cada instante la clepsidra deja caer la última gota.

DOOMSDAY

It will be when the trumpet sounds, as Saint John the
    theologian writes.
It was in 1757, according to Swedenborg.
It was in Israel (when the she-wolf nailed the flesh of Christ
    to the cross) but not only then.
It happens with every heartbeat.
There is no moment that can't be the pit of Hell.
There is no moment that can't be the water of Paradise.
There is no moment that isn't a loaded gun.
At any second you could be Cain or the Buddha, the mask or
    the face.
At any second Helen of Troy could reveal her love for you.
At any second the rooster could have crowed three times.
At every second the water clock lets fall the final drop.

—S.K.

MIDGARTHORMR

Sin fin el mar. Sin fin el pez, la verde
serpiente cosmogónica que encierra,
verde serpiente y verde mar, la tierra,
como ella circular. La boca muerde
la cola que le llega desde lejos,
desde el otro confín. El fuerte anillo
que nos abarca es tempestades, brillo,
sombra y rumor, reflejos de reflejos.
Es también la anfisbena. Eternamente
se miran sin horror los muchos ojos.
Cada cabeza husmea crasamente
los hierros de la guerra y los despojos.
Soñado fue en Islandia. Los abiertos
mares lo han divisado y lo han temido;
volverá con el barco maldecido
que se arma con las uñas de los muertos.
Alta será su inconcebible sombra
sobre la tierra pálida en el día
de altos lobos y espléndida agonía
del crepúsculo aquel que no se nombra.
Su imaginaria imagen nos mancilla.
Hacia el alba lo vi en la pesadilla.

MIDGARTHORMR

The sea without end. The fish without end, the green
cosmogonic serpent encircling everything,
green serpent and green ocean, and the earth,
like the ocean, circular. Its mouth is
biting its tail which arrives from a long way off,
from the other end. The mighty band
clasping us is storms, lightning flashes,
darkness and noise, reflections of reflections.
It is also the amphisbaena. Eternally
its many eyes stare at each other unafraid.
Each head sniffs stupidly
at the weapons of war and the slaughtered carcasses.
It was dreamed in Iceland. The open
seas have seen it and have feared it;
it will return with the ship of the damned
whose hull is plated with the toenails of the dead.
Its inconceivable shadow will tower
over the pale earth on the day
of tall wolves and dazzling agony
in that unspeakable twilight.
Its imaginary image leaves its stain on us.
I saw this in my nightmare before dawn.

—S.K.

INFERNO, V, 129

Dejan caer el libro, porque ya saben
que son las personas del libro.
(Lo serán de otro, el máximo,
pero eso qué puede importarles.)
Ahora son Paolo y Francesca,
no dos amigos que comparten
el sabor de una fábula.
Se miran con incrédula maravilla.
Las manos no se tocan.
Han descubierto el único tesoro;
han encontrado al otro.
No traicionan a Malatesta,
porque la traición requiere un tercero
y sólo existen ellos dos en el mundo.
Son Paolo y Francesca
y también la reina y su amante
y todos los amantes que han sido
desde aquel Adán y su Eva
en el pasto del Paraíso.
Un libro, un sueño les revela
que son formas de un sueño que fue soñado
en tierras de Bretaña.
Otro libro hará que los hombres,
sueños también, los sueñen.

INFERNO, V, 129

They drop the book when it grows clear to them
that the two people in the book are themselves.
(They'll be acting in another peerless one
but of what concern is that to them?)
Now they are Paolo and Francesca,
not two friends sharing
the sweet taste of a story.
Their eyes meet in wonder and disbelief.
Their hands do not touch.
They have discovered the sole treasure.
They have found the other.
They are not betraying Malatesta,
since betrayal requires a third party
and in the world just the two of them exist.
They are Paolo and Francesca
and also the queen and her lover
and all the lovers that ever were
since Adam lived with Eve
on the lawns of Paradise.
A book, a dream, has made them see
that they are creatures of a dream once dreamt
in Breton lands.
Another book will see to it that men,
also, will dream their dreams of them.

—A.S.T.

ELEGÍA DE UN PARQUE

Se perdió el laberinto. Se perdieron
todos los eucaliptos ordenados,
los toldos del verano y la vigilia
del incesante espejo, repitiendo
cada expresión de cada rostro humano,
cada fugacidad. El detenido
reloj, la entretejida madreselva,
la glorieta, las frívolas estatuas,
el otro lado de la tarde, el trino,
el mirador y el ocio de la fuente
son cosas del pasado. ¿Del pasado?
Si no hubo un principio ni habrá un término,
si nos aguarda una infinita suma
de blancos días y de negras noches,
ya somos el pasado que seremos.
Somos el tiempo, el río indivisible,
somos Uxmal, Cartago y la borrada
muralla del romano y el perdido
parque que conmemoran estos versos.

ELEGY FOR A PARK

The labyrinth has vanished. Vanished also
those orderly avenues of eucalyptus,
the summer awnings, and the watchful eye
of the ever-seeing mirror, duplicating
every expression on every human face,
everything brief and fleeting. The stopped clock,
the ingrown tangle of the honeysuckle,
the garden arbor with its whimsical statues,
the other side of evening, the trill of birds,
the mirador, the lazy swish of a fountain,
are all things of the past. Things of what past?
If there were no beginning, nor imminent ending,
if lying in store for us is an infinity
of white days alternating with black nights,
we are living now the past we will become.
We are time itself, the indivisible river.
We are Uxmal and Carthage, we are the perished
walls of the Romans and the vanished park,
the vanished park these lines commemorate.

— A.R.

HAIKU

La vasta noche
no es ahora otra cosa
que una fragancia.

.

¿Es o no es
el sueño que olvidé
antes del alba?

.

La ociosa espada
sueña con sus batallas.
Otro es mi sueño.

.

El hombre ha muerto.
La barba no lo sabe.
Crecen las uñas.

HAIKU

The endless night
is now nothing more
than a scent.

•

Is it or isn't it
the dream I forgot
before dawn?

•

The sword at rest
dreams of its battles.
My dream is something else.

•

The man has died.
His beard doesn't know.
His nails keep growing.

Bajo la luna
la sombra que se alarga
es una sola.

*

La vieja mano
sigue trazando versos
para el olvido.

Under the moon
the lengthening shadow
is all one shadow.

.

The old hand
goes on setting down lines
for oblivion.

—s.k.

LA CIFRA

La amistad silenciosa de la luna
(cito mal a Virgilio) te acompaña
desde aquella perdida hoy en el tiempo
noche o atardecer en que tus vagos
ojos la descifraron para siempre
en un jardín o un patio que son polvo.
¿Para siempre? Yo sé que alguien, un día,
podrá decirte verdaderamente:
"No volverás a ver la clara luna,
Has agotado ya la inalterable
suma de veces que te da el destino.
Inútil abrir todas las ventanas
del mundo. Es tarde. No darás con ella."
Vivimos descubriendo y olvidando
esa dulce costumbre de la noche.
Hay que mirarla bien. Puede ser última.

THE LIMIT

The silent friendship of the moon
(I misquote Virgil) has kept you company
since that one night or evening
now lost in time, when your restless
eyes first made her out for always
in a patio or a garden since gone to dust.
For always? I know that someday someone
will find a way of telling you this truth:
"You'll never see the moon aglow again.
You've now attained the limit set for you
by destiny. No use opening every window
throughout the world. Too late. You'll never find her."
Our life is spent discovering and forgetting
that gentle habit of the night.
Take a good look. It could be the last.

—A.S.T.

MILONGA DEL MUERTO

Lo he soñado en esta casa
entre paredes y puertas.
Dios les permite a los hombres
soñar cosas que son ciertas.

Lo he soñado mar afuera
en unas islas glaciales.
Que nos digan lo demás
la tumba y los hospitales.

Una de tantas provincias
del interior fue su tierra.
(No conviene que se sepa
que muere gente en la guerra.)

Lo sacaron del cuartel,
le pusieron en las manos
las armas y lo mandaron
a morir con sus hermanos.

Se obró con suma prudencia,
se habló de un modo prolijo.
Les entregaron a un tiempo
el rifle y el crucifijo.

Oyó las vanas arengas
de los vanos generales.
Vio lo que nunca había visto,
la sangre en los arenales.

JORGE LUIS BORGES

MILONGA OF THE DEAD MAN

I dreamed it inside this house
in between walls and doors.
God allows man to dream
things that are surely true.

I dreamed it out at sea
among floating islands of ice.
May we be told the rest
by hospitals and tombs.

One of so many provinces
of the interior was his land.
(It is not worth our knowing
that people die in war.)

They took him out of the barracks,
put weapons in his hands
and then gave him the order
to die among his brothers.

He acted with great discretion,
he talked to himself at length.
At one and the same time
they gave him a gun and a cross.

He heard the vain harangues
of the vain generals.
He saw what he'd never seen,
blood on the sandy ground.

Oyó vivas y oyó mueras,
oyó el clamor de la gente.
Él sólo quería saber
si era o si no era valiente.

Lo supo en aquel momento
en que le entraba la herida.
Se dijo *No tuve miedo*
cuando lo dejó la vida.

Su muerte fue una secreta
victoria. Nadie se asombre
de que me dé envidia y pena
el destino de aquel hombre.

JORGE LUIS BORGES

He heard the people shouting
Long live! and Let them die!
All he wanted to know
was whether or not he was brave.

He knew it the very instant
the bullet entered his body.
He said *I wasn't afraid*
as life abandoned him.

His death was a secret victory.
No one should be surprised
that I feel envy and sorrow
for that man's destiny.

—s.k.

EL DON

En una página de Plinio se lee
que en todo el orbe no hay dos caras iguales.
Una mujer le dio a un ciego la imagen
de su rostro, sin duda único.
Eligió la fotografía entre muchas;
descartó y acertó.
El acto fue significativo para ella
y también lo es para él.
Ella sabía que él no podía ver el regalo
y sabía que era un regalo.
Un invisible don es un hecho mágico.
Dar a un ciego una imagen
es dar algo tan tenue que bien puede ser infinito,
es dar algo tan vago que puede ser el universo.
La inútil mano toca y no reconoce
la inalcanzable cara.

En revista Maldoror, *Montevideo, Nº 20, 1985.*

THE GIFT

In a page of Pliny we read
that in all the world no two faces are alike.
A woman gave a blind man
the image of her face,
without a doubt unique.
She chose the photo among many;
rejected all but one and got it right.
The act had meaning for her
as it does for him.
She knew he could not see her gift
and knew it was a present.
An invisible gift is an act of magic.
To give a blind man an image
is to give something so tenuous it can be infinite
something so vague it can be the universe.
The useless hand touches
and does not recognize
the unreachable face.

—C.M.

APPENDIX

INSOMNIO

Resulta legendariamente chica y lejana aquella etapa donde los
   relojes vertieron la media noche absoluta.
Estos seis muros estrechos llenos de eternidad estrecha me
   ahogan.
Y en el cráneo sigue vibrando esta lamentable llama de
   alcohol que no quiere apagarse.
Que no puede apagarse.
Reducción al absurdo del problema de la inmortalidad del
   espíritu.
Me he desangrado en demasiados ponientes.
La ventana sintetiza el gesto solitario del farol.
Apergaminado y plausible film cinemático.
La ventana imanta todas las ojeadas inquietas.
Cómo me ahorcan las cuerdas del horizonte.
¿Llueve? ¿Qué morfina inyectarán a las calles esas agujas?
No.
Son girones [sic] vagos de siglos que gotean isócronos del
   cielo raso.
Es la letanía lenta de la sangre.
Son los dientes de la obscuridad que roen las paredes.
Bajo los párpados ondean y se apagan nuevamente las
   tempestades rotas.
Los días son todos de papel azul bien cortaditos por la misma
   tijera sobre el agujero inexistente del Cosmos.
El recuerdo enciende una lámpara:
*Otra vez arrastramos con nosotros esa calle que la ropa
   tendida embanderó tan jubilosamente.*
Muy lejos se hundió el frondoso piano del tupi.
El sol ventilador vertiginoso tumba los caserones.
*Al vernos navegar tan espirales se ríen a carcajadas las
   puertas.*
Pedro-Luis me confía: —Yo soy un hombre bueno, Jorge.

JORGE LUIS BORGES

INSOMNIA

It seems legendarily small and remote, that epoch when
    the clocks
spilled out absolute midnight.
I feel suffocated by these six narrow walls full of narrow
    eternity.
In the skull, a lambent, lamentable flame of alcohol that
    refuses to go out.
That cannot be put out.
Reductio ad absurdum of the problem of the immortality of
    the spirit.
I have bled into too many sunsets.
The window synthesizes the solitary gesture of the streetlamp.
Plausible movie wrinkled like parchment.
The window pulls like a magnet on all the restless glances.
I am hanged on the ropes of the horizon.
Is it raining? What morphine can those needles be injecting
    into the streets?
No.
They are vague tatters of centuries falling together from the
    ceiling.
It is the slow litany of the blood.
The teeth of darkness gnawing at the walls.
Under the eyelids, shreds of storm undulate and splutter.
The days are blue paper, all nicely cut by the same scissor,
    over the inexistent gap of the Cosmos.
Memory turns on a lamp:
Once again we drag behind us that street gaily festooned
    with clothes hung out to dry.
Submerged, far away, the leafy piano of the Tupi.
The sun, dizzily spinning fan, knocks over the big old houses.
And doors burst out laughing to see us trace such spirals.
Pedro-Luis confesses: "I am a good man, Jorge."

Tu eres un hombre bueno, Jorge . . . Ya se nos pasará
    tomando una tacita de café.
Los ojos estallan cuando los golpean las aspas del sol.
¿Qué hangar cobijará definitivamente las emociones?
Sin duda existe un plano ultra-espacial donde todas ellas son
    formas de una fuerza utilizable y sujeta.
Como el agua y la electricidad en este plano.
Ira. Anarquismo. Hambre sexual.
Artificio para hacernos vibrar mágicamente.
Ninguna piedra rompe la noche.
Ninguna mano aviva las cenizas del incendio de todos los
    estandartes.

*Grecia, Madrid, Año 3, N° 49, 15 de septiembre de 1920.

JORGE LUIS BORGES

You are a good man, Jorge . . . We'll make up for it
    with a nice cup of coffee.
The eyes burst when hit by the blades of the sun.
What hangar will give definitive shelter to the emotions?
No doubt there is a level beyond space where they are all
    forms whose strength can be bent to use.
Like water and electricity down here.
Anger. Anarchy. Sexual hunger.
Artifice to make us vibrate magically.
No stone breaks the night.
No hand stirs the embers of all the banners.

—C.M.

UN PATIO

Con la tarde
se cansaron los dos o tres colores del patio.
Esta noche, la luna, el claro círculo,
no domina su espacio.
Patio, cielo encauzado.
El patio es el declive
por el cual se derrama el cielo en la casa.
Serena,
la eternidad espera en la encrucijada de estrellas.
Grato es vivir en la amistad oscura
de un zaguán, de una parra y de un aljibe.

PATIO

With evening
the two or three colors of the patio grew weary.
Tonight, the moon's bright circle
does not dominate outer space.
Patio, heaven's watercourse.
The patio is the slope
down which the sky flows into the house.
Serenely,
eternity waits at the crossway of the stars.
It is lovely to live in the dark friendliness
of covered entranceway, arbor, and wellhead.

—R.F.

JORGE LUIS BORGES

INSCRIPCIÓN SEPULCRAL

Para mi bisabuelo, el coronel Isidoro Suárez

Dilató su valor sobre los Andes.
Contrastó montañas y ejércitos.
La audacia fue costumbre de su espada.
Impuso en la llanura de Junín
término venturoso a la batalla
y a las lanzas del Perú dio sangre española.
Escribió su censo de hazañas
en prosa rígida como los clarines belísonos.
Eligió el honroso destierro.
Ahora es un poco de ceniza y de gloria.

SEPULCHRAL INSCRIPTION

For my great-grandfather Isidoro Suárez

His valor passed beyond the Andes.
He fought against mountains and armies.
Audacity was a habit with his sword.
On the plain at Junín he put
a lucky end to the fight
and gave Spanish blood to Peruvian lances.
He wrote his roll of deeds
in prose inflexible as battlesinging trumpets.
He chose an honorable exile.
Now he is a handful of dust and glory.

—R.F.

Notes

I. A POET DREAMS (1922–1957)

p. 15 Afterglow: The last two lines of the poem paraphrase a fragment from Novalis that Borges translated in 1934. See Borges, Jorge Luis, *Obras, reseñas y traducciones inéditas. Diario Crítica. 1933–1934*, Irma Zangara (ed.), Buenos Aires, Editorial Atlántida, 1995, p. 278.

p. 17 Sepulchral Inscription: "The most romantic of all Borges's ancestors was undoubtedly Isidoro Suárez, a great-grandfather on his mother's side. At the age of twenty-four, Suárez led the cavalry charge that turned the tide of battle at Junín, the second-last engagement in the liberation of South America. The battle took place on August 6, 1824, high up in the Andes of Peru," Edwin Williamson, *Borges: A Life*, New York, Viking, p. 3.

p. 23 General Quiroga Rides to His Death in a Carriage: The *gaucho caudillo* Juan Facundo Quiroga (1788–1835), the protagonist of Domingo Faustino Sarmiento's *Facundo*—considered by Borges to be the undisputed classic of nineteenth-century Argentine literature—was assassinated. Sarmiento accused agents of the strong-man and dictator Juan Manuel Rosas (1793–1877) of being the perpetrators.

p. 41 The Cyclical Night: Laprida, Cabrera, Soler, and Suárez—ancestors of Borges—are all figures of Argentine history. Jerónimo de Cabrera was a conquistador; Isidoro Suárez and Miguel Estanislao Soler fought in the wars of South American independence from Spain; and Francisco Laprida was president of the congress that declared the independence of what would later become the Argentine nation. See Edwin Williamson's *Borges: A Life*, pp. 3–16.

p. 45 Conjectural Poem: "Arriva' io forato ne la gola / fuggendo a piede e sanguinando il piano." ("I came wounded in the throat, fleeing on foot and bloodying the plain"), *The Divine Comedy*, V, 98–99, Dante, *Purgatorio*, Charles S. Singleton, Princeton University

Press, 1989, p. 50. See also note 24 of the introduction to *Poems of the Night*.

p. 53 **Museum:** According to Nestor Ibarra, the poems that make up "Museum" (of which we include ones associated to the theme of this book) are apocryphal translations intended to be read as translations. Borges wanted to produce the effect of the reader dealing with translations that are too literal. See Ibarra's note to his own French translation of "Museum" in Jorge Luis Borges, *Oeuvre poétique, 1925–1965*, Paris, Gallimard, 1985, p. 203.

II. THE GIFT OF BLINDNESS (1958–1977)

p. 57 **Poem of the Gifts:** Paul Groussac (1845–1929) moved to Buenos Aires from his native France in 1866. He wrote books in French and Spanish. He was director of Argentina's National Library from 1885 to 1929. He lost his sight in 1925 due to an illness. Borges identifies with Groussac, but modestly exaggerates the parallel to his own situation: whereas Groussac lost his sight a few years before his death, Borges went blind in 1955, and unlike Groussac he continued an active literary career. Readers of Borges's short stories might be interested to know that the building that housed Argentina's national library during Borges's tenure as national librarian had previously housed Argentina's national lottery.

p. 61 **The Moon:** In this poem Borges aludes to a famous line by the Spanish poet Francisco de Quevedo (1580–1645), which he also quotes in "To an Old Poet," a sonnet that imagines the aging poet. In Stephen Kessler's translation of "To an Old Poet," the line reads: *And his epitaph the blood-soaked moon ("y su epitafio la sangrienta luna")*.

Borges also mentions the Argentine man of letters Leopoldo Lugones (1874–1938), who wrote *Lunario sentimental* (1909), an influential book of poems (and some short texts in other genres) focusing entirely on the moon. In his youth Borges had been somewhat critical of Lugones, but he reconsidered the significance of his distinguished antecedent. In 1938 he called him the greatest Argentine writer, and dedicated *The Maker* (1960) to him. For the vicissitudes of Borges's views on Lugones, see Balderston, Daniel, Gastón Gallo and Nicolás Helft, *Borges, una encyclopedia*, Buenos Aires, Norma, 1999, pp. 209–212.

p. 91 **Where Can They Have Gone?:** This poem comes from the brief collection *For Six Strings* included in *The Self and the Other*

(1964), which evoke Argentine popular themes. Juan Moreira was a character in popular theater, Juan Muraña was a legendary knife-fighter from Buenos Aires, and the brothers Iberra are characters in "Milonga de dos hermanos," a poem by Borges in which two Argentine knife-fighters recreate the story of Cain and Abel. According to Jean Pierre Bernès, Borges remembered the Iberra brothers as cattle-robbers who became the bodyguards of local caudillos. See the note by Bernès in Jorge Luis Borges, *Oeuvres complètes II*, Paris, Gallimard, 1999, p. 1233.

p. 99 **Two Versions of "Knight, Death, and the Devil":** Borges owned a reproduction of Dürer's print years before he lost his sight.

p. 103 **In Praise of Darkness:** Retiro and Recoleta are two upscale neighborhoods in Buenos Aires. Recoleta is also the name of Buenos Aires's most prestigious cemetery.

p. 107 **The Gold of the Tigers:** NOTE BY BORGES: "For the ring of the nine nights the curious reader can interrogate chapter 49 of the *Prose Edda*. The name of the ring is Draupnir," Borges, Jorge Luis, *Obra poética*, p. 387. Borges is referring to the *Gilfaginning*, the section of the *Prose Edda* he translated as *La alucinación de Gylfi* (Gilfy's Hallucination). In chapter 49, Borges translates the description of the great golden ring called Draupnir: "This was its virtue: every ninth night eight golden rings of the same weight would drop from it," Snorri Sturluson, *La alucinación de Gylfi* (Gilfy's Hallucination), Madrid, Alianza Editorial, 1984, p. 92.

p. 113 **Elegy:** NOTE BY BORGES: "Scyld is the king of Denmark whose destiny is sung in the exordium to the Saga of Beowulf. The beautiful and dead god is Baldr, whose prophetic dreams and whose end are in the *Eddas*," Borges, *Obra poética*, p. 436.

p. 117 **Ein Traum:** NOTE BY BORGES: "Ein Traum was dictated to me in a morning in East Lansing without my understanding it, and without any sensible disquiet; I was able to transcribe it later, word by word. It is, needless to say, a mere psychological curiosisty, or if the reader is very generous, an inoffensive parable of solipsisim," Borges, *Obra poética*, p. 476.

p. 119 **Signs:** NOTE BY BORGES: "Some five hundred years before the Christian Era someone wrote: '*Chuang-Tzu dreamt he was a butterfly, and when he awoke he did not know if he was the man who dreamt he was a butterfly, or a butterfly who now dreamt he was a man,*'" Borges, *Obra poética*, p. 523.

p. 125 **I Am Not Even Dust:** Urganda, the fairy, and Amadis the hero are characters from *Amadis de Gaula*, a Spanish novel of chivalry first published in 1508. Alonso Quijano will become Don Quixote in Cervantes's masterpiece.

p. 131 **Adam Is Your Ashes:** General Justo José de Urquiza—the third president of Argentina—was the caudillo who deposed the dictator Juan Manuel Rosas in 1852 in the battle of Caseros.

III. WAITING FOR THE NIGHT (1978–1985)

p. 135 **History of the Night:** Fray Luis de León (1527–1591), a theologian, biblical translator, and one of the great poets of the Spanish Golden Age, was imprisoned by the Spanish inquisition for his translation of the "Song of Songs." In prison he wrote his most famous poetic lines.

p. 137 **The Young Night:** Borges discussed the line by Goethe quoted in the poem: "*Alles Nähe werde fern*, everything near becomes far. Goethe was referring to the evening twilight. Everything near becomes far. It is true. At nightfall, the closest to us seems to move away from our eyes. So the visible world has moved away from my eyes, perhaps forever. Goethe could be referring not only to twilight but to life. All things go off, leaving us. Old age is probably the supreme solitude—except that the supreme solitude is death. And 'everything near becomes far' also refers to the slow process of blindness which is not a complete misfortune. It is one more instrument among the many—all of them strange—that fate or chance provide," "Blindness," *Selected Non-Fictions* (edited by Eliot Weinberger), New York, Penguin, 1999, p. 483.

p. 145 **Yesterdays:** See note for "Two Versions of 'Knight, Death, and the Devil.'"

p. 155 **The Horse:** NOTE BY BORGES: "I must correct a quotation. Chaucer (*The Squires Tale*, 194) wrote: *Therwith so horsly, and so quik of yë*," Borges, *Obra poética*, p. 522.

p. 161 **Midgarthormr:** In Nordic Mythology Midgarthormr is the serpent that surrounds the world biting its own tail. The serpent is one of the animals unleashed during the Ragnarök (the Old Norse twilight of the gods). The god Thor will slaughter the serpent, but he will die from its poison. This prophecy is described in chapter 51 of the *Gilfaginning*. See p. 99 in Borges's translation (quoted in note for #32).

p. 163 *Inferno*, V, 129: "Noi leggiavamo un giorno per diletto / di Lancialotto come amor lo strinse; / sole eravamo e sanza alcun *sospetto.*" ("One day, for pastime, we read Lancelot, how love constrained him; *we were alone, suspecting nothing.*") V, 127–129, Dante, *The Divine Comedy*, translated by Charles S. Singleton, Princeton University Press, 1989, pp. 50–51. We have underlined the line referenced in Borges's title (*Inferno*, V 129) in both the Italian and the English.

p. 177 The Gift: "Although our faces or features contain ten or so characteristics, no two faces exist among all the thousands of human beings that cannot be differentiated—a situation that no form of art could aspire to achieve." Pliny the Elder, *Natural History*, Book VII, no. 6, p. 75, John F. Healy (editor and translator), New York, Penguin, 1991.

APPENDIX

p. 181 Insomnia: 1—"Pedro-Luis" mentioned in the poem was Pedro-Luis de Gálvez, an avant-garde poet (eighteen years his senior) Borges befriended in Spain. According to Edwin Williamson, "Gálvez embodied a marvelous combination of poet and adventurer that a timid youth like Georgie must have found irresistible. The young Borges thought there was a touch of genius in the man. Gálvez's work, which consisted of sonnets for the most part, was characterized by startling images and fierce passions, and it was this conjunction of violent emotion and formal constraint that may so have attracted Borges at this time," *Borges: A Life*, p. 72.

Sources

(SP): *Selected Poems*, Edited by Alexander Coleman, New York, Penguin, 1999.

(OP): *Obra poética*, Buenos Aires, Emecé, 2008.

(SP 1923–1967): *Selected Poems 1923–1967*, Edited by Norman Thomas di Giovanni, New York, Penguin, 1985.

(OC): *Obras completas* (1975–1985), Barcelona, Emecé, 1989.

(A): *Atlas*, Translated by Anthony Kerrigan, New York, E. P. Dutton, 1985.

(TR 1919–1929): *Textos recobrados (1919–1929)*, Buenos Aires, Emecé, 1999.

(TR 1956–1986): *Textos recobrados (1956–1986)*, Buenos Aires, Emecé, 2003.

The poems are listed below, grouped under the title of the book in which they first appeared in Spanish. The right-hand column gives the abbreviation of the edition from which originals and translations are drawn. New translations are denoted by an asterisk.

From *Fervor de Buenos Aires* (1923)

Patio	(SP 1923–1967)
Un patio	(SP 1923–1967)
Sepulchral Inscription	(SP 1923–1967)
Inscripción sepulcral	(SP 1923–1967)
Remorse for Any Death	(SP)
Remordimiento por cualquier muerte	(SP)
Inscription on Any Tomb	(SP)

From *The Self and the Other* (1964)
Insomnia*
Insomnio   (OP)
The Cyclical Night   (SP)
La noche cíclica   (SP)
Of Heaven and Hell   (SP)
Del infierno y del cielo   (SP)
Conjectural Poem   (SP)
Poema conjetural   (SP)
Limits   (SP)
Límites   (SP)
The Golem   (SP)
El golem   (SP)
Someone   (SP)
Alguien   (SP)

From *For Six Strings* (1965)
Where Can They Have Gone?   (SP)
¿Dónde se habrán ido?   (SP)

From *In Praise of Darkness* (1969)
Heraclitus*
Heráclito   (OP)
The Labyrinth   (SP 1923–1967)
El Laberinto   (SP 1923–1967)
Two versions of "Knight, Death, and the Devil" (SP)
Dos versiones de "Ritter, Tod und Teufel" (SP)
In Praise of Darkness   (SP)
Elogio de la sombra   (SP)

From *The Gold of the Tigers* (1972)
The Gold of the Tigers   (SP)
El oro de los tigres   (SP)

From *The Unending Rose* (1975)
The Dream   (SP)
El sueño   (SP)
The Suicide   (SP)
El suicida   (SP)

From *Atlas* (1984)
    A Nightmare   (A)
    Una pesadilla   (OC)
    Dreams   (A)
    Los sueños   (OC)

From *Los Conjurados* (1985)
    Doomsday*
    Doomsday   (OP)
    The Young Night*
    La joven noche   (OP)
    Elegy for a Park   (SP)
    Elegía de un parque   (SP)
    Someone Will Dream*
    Alguien soñará   (OP)
    Midgarthormr*
    Midgarthormr   (OP)
    A Dream in Edinburgh*
    Sueño soñado en Edimburgo   (OP)
    Milonga of the Dead Man*
    Milonga del muerto   (OP)

From *Textos Recobrados* (1919–1929)
    Insomnia* (1921)
    Insomnio (1921)   (TR 1919–1929)

From *Textos Recobrados* (1956–1986)
    The Gift*
    El don   (TR 1956–1986)

Index

Titles in English

Titles in Spanish

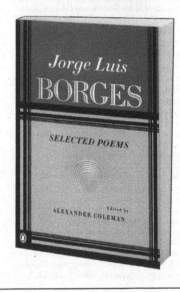